Soul Fruit

Bearing Blessings through Cancer

By

Dr. Rev. Scott T. Arnold

8 Fulton St.
Quincy, Michigan 49082

Scotteagle7@aol.com

1

The design of the front cover
was made by Scott Arnold when
he was an art student at Delta College,
University Center, Michigan.

Title of design:
"The Four Seasons"
Acrylic
1978

Soul Fruit
Bearing Blessings through Cancer

Outline:

Please note that Scriptural references indicated by the initials "NIV" will be from the New International Version, published by the Zondervan Company. 1983

This book is dedicated to my brother, Dr. Bruce Arnold, who exemplified courage and faith as he battled cancer. May his trumpet brightly resound in heaven!
I also thank God for my wonderful wife Marilyn, our three sons Mark, Thom, and John, and for our supportive families, including the Union Church of Quincy, Michigan.

1. Blessings through Cancer
(Adversity is the ground for soul fruit)

On June 13th, 2005, I woke up with my heart strongly moved in prayer. God had spoken to me to write this book on the blessings we can discover while dealing with cancer. My first thought was "Lord, I woke up today with a son in the hospital fighting for his life with cancer, and right now you are planting this seed of writing a book on the blessings that come through fighting cancer?" This was one of those times when a "not so gentle" wrestle within my soul could only be resolved by allowing doubt to give way to trust. Being a cancer survivor myself, God had helped me to discover how cancer and many other illnesses and trials are a challenging call for faith. It can be hard to see the blessings of God in the midst of a storm of concerns. So I asked God, "How will I find the strength and resources to write this?" After listening to the Lord's leading, I realized that God's prompting to write this book was a revelation of hope. He was calling me to a future time that would involve sharing the blessings that have come through fighting cancer. God moved in a merciful and mysterious way to encourage us as we faced this crisis. Now, over three years later, I am grateful to share our story and the blessings that have come through what we have learned about life and our loving Creator.

Thom had just gone through two weeks of emergency, life-threatening, intervention. In fact, they had discovered a large cancerous tumor in his chest the size of a football. The situation was critical, the implications and prognosis were beyond fathoming. We wondered if Thom was going to make it. Death was a specter that we were facing. This was a time for courage amidst fears and tears, a trial that challenged our faith. The doctors struggled with knowing how to treat him. In our minds we remembered my own battle with cancer, two years before, but this time it was different. The fast growing cancer had brought on an immediate life-threatening crisis. One might expect to face cancer in mid-life or in old age, but to see your child face cancer and watch him battle it while being on the edge of his life and breath was both overwhelming and emotionally painful.

Prayers had gone up from many people as they prayed that God would work to provide help and healing for our son. Yet with the stress of the last two weeks that involved the discovery and aggressive treatment of our son's cancer, neither we, nor the doctors, were in a position to know what would eventually happen to him. His tumor had grown to almost completely block his airway and was advanced enough to cause his lungs to be filled with fluid. From the rush that surrounded his being airlifted by helicopter to University of Michigan Hospital, to the intervention of doctors who drained suffocating fluid from his lungs by inserting chest tubes without anesthesia in both lungs, to the measures taken to insert a pericardial drain tube and monitor his heart, we saw how God used a team of doctors and nurses to help him survive his first two weeks of emergency treatment. We observed how God gave him incredible courage and strength. We had banded together in prayer, watching, encouraging, waiting, and hoping.

While I remained silent early morning on June 13th, I was open to God as I prayed. I remembered how I had thought in the back of my mind, just days before while coping with our crisis, that some day we would make it through this and we would be able to bless others in sharing our story. I held on to the seed of hope that God had given us, even though we were in the midst of many challenges. We were being called to become fully reliant upon the promise and hope of God's grace while realizing the seriousness of his cancer. Little did I know the many ways that God would work to bless us all on this day, June 13th, Thom's 16th birthday. We were hopeful yet we were concerned, worn-out and anxious. Marilyn and I, Thom's brothers Mark and John, and our immediate family and friends, had gone through tremendous grief. Was this treatable? Would he survive? What would we face in the days and weeks to come? It was difficult to think past the immediate problem, and it was difficult to know what the upcoming battle with cancer would entail. What would the outcome from all this be?

With a mixture of feelings, and a desire to be responsive to God's leading, I began to study scripture and log on to my laptop that morning. God began to show me a clear connection. God blesses us through the tough times of life by growing and nurturing the fruit of the Spirit in our lives (Galatians 5:22-23). Quite often adversity in life is the ground for soul fruit within us that is born of God's Spirit giving us strength and character. The scripture that contained a definition of faith came from Hebrews 11:1, and it touched my heart and soul with blessed counsel: *"Now faith is being sure of what we hope for and certain of what we do not see."* With this inspiration I began to type, letting the response of faith within my soul run through my fingers into an outline on my laptop. I rejoiced in the hope of God's Word that called for us to be strong in faith, hope, and love. I felt the positive presence and direction of the Holy Spirit of God. I packed up my briefcase, had breakfast with our youngest son John (13 at the time) and we proceeded to join Thom and Marilyn at the hospital. The theme "a day of blessing" would be affirmed throughout Thom's birthday. The precious gift of life would be accentuated in this crucible experience in which health concerns would be overcome by a celebration of God's grace and hope.

In arriving at the hospital, Thom was glad to see us. Marilyn once again had watched over him faithfully overnight. While Thom had been worked on by a steady stream of doctors and specialists, he expressed his hope that it would be a great birthday. He wondered who might come to celebrate with him. He was expectantly hopeful.

7

His tests, procedures, and chemotherapy treatments kept him occupied early on in the day. The steroids were making him a little edgy. However, by 11:00 a.m., the activity of the medical treatments had settled down, and a lady knocked at the door representing a sister church of ours in this university town of Ann Arbor. She had heard of Thom and was very gracious and prayed that God would bless Thom on his birthday. Right after the she left, our oncologist Dr. Linda McAllister-Lucas came in and encouraged Thom, and promised to give him a book of his choice as a birthday gift. Walking in soon afterward, and standing by Dr. McAllister's side, was a woman who held a big bundle of colorful helium balloons. Dr. McAllister introduced us to a lady named Val. She had heard of Thom through our church's regional association and had brought his health concern to her own church's prayer chain.

Val began to share her story with us. With transparent openness she shared of how her daughter had fought cancer here at Mott Children's Hospital. Expressing her faith and joy in the Lord, she went on to say that her daughter had lived for two more years after her battle with cancer began. We were moved by Val's compassion that led her to drive some distance to come and visit Thom. She went on to say that she had learned through her experience that God would always be with us, no matter what would come our way. While her daughter's cancer was different, and Val spoke of death in a way that involved courage and faith, her testimony spoke to us of the very truth we needed to hold on to. Val looked directly to us and said: "The greatest blessing I can share with you today is to affirm God's presence. He will be with you always. Jesus said 'I will never leave you nor forsake you.' My daughter and I were so blessed to share two years of faith together, God did amazing and wonderful things in those two years, and I have come today to let you know that there are blessings God gives to us when we go through these things." There was much more that Val shared with us, but most of all she shared her faith, hope, and love in Christ. "In all this", she said, "God is Sovereign, and is not taken by surprise." Her presence and words were a ministry of love, a blessing that came unexpectedly as God used one of His many messengers that day. Val helped to remind us that whatever we would face, even in the midst of this battle with cancer, the truth of God being with us was evident and encouraging. God used her to help us be confident in faith and hope. Our faith focus brightened as this day went on, a growing joy from the Lord that was being revealed as we experienced a series of blessings. This began an outpouring of encouragement that day, fruit from God's Spirit.

Around noon, Thom's birthday became even more special. He was surprised by the arrival of his cousins who drove from Chicago to celebrate his birthday, as they came in with our oldest son Mark (19 at the time). The look on Thom's face was filled with child-like joy and gratitude as he saw their faces beyond another large bundle of balloons that they were carrying. Within an hour, his uncle Doming and cousin Denise surprised him, arriving from Arkansas. My brother Paul (a pastor of a nearby church) and his family then also arrived with pizza. Soon afterward, fifteen friends from church and school arrived, having driven 50 miles. They carried in gifts and cakes, and the hospital pediatric oncology unit was charged with life as laughter and smiles were mixed with tears. Thom looked at all his friends, family, and the birthday cakes, three in all, and said: "Enjoy the cake, I give my cancer blessings." Thom's good natured humor shined through. We all sang happy birthday, our hearts were touched deeply. I would normally have said a prayer, but being choked up by the joy of God's presence with us I asked Paul to pray. He said: "Thank you Lord for the great blessing of Thom, and your presence with us today, and of the blessing of friends and family."

In this prayer, and through this joyful experience, the revelation of God blessing us was clear and profound.

Thom began opening the many cards and gifts that were brought from the church, and were given by his friends. Dr. McAllister walked in again and commented: "Thom, you are so blessed with friends. People must really like you." Thom responded: "Yes, I know I am blessed." As Thom's friends were about to leave, my wife Marilyn looked at me and said: "Say something before they go." I looked around the room as I felt gratitude to God for their presence. Thom was indeed blessed, and so were we, to have them as his friends. Then I said: "The blessing of life and friendship is something that has been shared in a beautiful way today. But I hope that each of you may know that the greatest friend is the Savior Jesus Christ. Our lives are eternally blessed if we know Him." This was a moment of grace and truth. As family and friends, we were touched with an awareness of God's presence and power, there was an awareness of how God's grace and love were at work to unite us in that moment. There was a burning glow in our hearts, one that would show in our faces and shine from our lives.

An hour later, when all the wonderful birthday celebrations had subsided, I was helping my brother-in-law Doming check in to the hospital inn, when I overheard him whistle: "Count Your Blessings". I smiled as I realized the many ways God had blessed this day, and affirmed the need for this book to be written. As the quiet moments of the day's end came, Thom and I reflected about how wonderful a day it was, even though he was in the hospital fighting cancer. He was grateful and felt blessed and surrounded by the love of God. He then said: "I think everyone should have a time like this to appreciate life and to grow in faith." The words of the great hymn whistled by Doming earlier in the day began to speak truth in my heart with the prompting of Thom's revelation. *"Count your many blessings, name them one by one. Count your many blessings see what God has done."* Thom said good night to us, he rested in the peace of knowing that God was with him, and that family and friends loved him. We affirmed that life is filled with blessings, hope, and peace even while dealing with cancer. As a father, I could not have imagined the great blessings God would reveal to us that day. I still weep with joy upon remembering the goodness and grace of God which was poured out to us in abundance.

In reflection that night, I thought back to my own experience of fighting cancer which helped me to relate to Thom. Two years prior, God had worked in many mighty and miraculous ways to heal me, and bless us through my own experience of cancer. God is good, and we must learn to trust in His sovereign will that is at work in all things.

Cancer is a disease, and blessings can be discovered when facing disease, trials, or troubles in life. I am not saying that cancer as a disease is the blessing, what I am saying is that we can experience God's blessing while dealing with cancer or any other illness. Likewise, we can experience the strength of loving communities and the blessings of love shared through cancer. Ultimately all of us need a greater healing and hope. The redemption and transformation of our souls (salvation) is the gift of God's grace that we need in order to be delivered from our corruptibility and mortality. The greatest hope for healing is in the resurrection power of Jesus Christ. In Jesus Christ I have found forgiveness, love, truth, new life, healing and hope. Cancer can serve as a reminder of our humanity. Our lives are fragile. We may seek the blessing of God in the hard times or we can become bitter. In the midst of our battles with cancer, we have chosen the path of faith, the way of trusting in Jesus Christ.

In this book I pray that you will join me to explore how we can find blessings while fighting cancer with faith and hope in God. For those who struggle with faith in God, may these words of encouragement help you find inner strength and an awareness of support from those who are your own network of care. Though you may not embrace or accept the idea that God is at work, and provides you people to help you, I ask that you listen to my story and begin to look at your life in a new way. I can testify that God blesses people who fight cancer with faith and the fruit of the Spirit. Paul listed what the fruit of the Spirit were as he wrote a letter to the Galatians: Love, Joy, Peace, Patience, Kindness, Goodness, Faithfulness, Gentleness, and Self-Control. Such fruit is often born through adversity.

There have been many hurdles to overcome in writing this book, but even these have served to intensify the testimony of God's grace and truthful presence. God is able to help you, and it is up to each of us to believe and trust in Him. We are even called to function as the supportive community that God so designed for help in facing hardships and illness. Cancer is a reminder and stimulus for such love to be expressed unselfishly. The words of Jesus bless and encourage this faith: *"I have told you these things, so that in me you may have peace. In this world you will have trouble. But take heart! I have overcome the world."* (John 16:33 NIV) No matter what a person may be confronted with, even cancer, be sure of this promise: You can overcome cancer, death, loneliness, grief, loss, illness, addiction, anything, if you know the Great Physician and Savior Jesus Christ.

Overcoming cancer, or any other disease in this life, involves more than chasing after a cure. Healing will not always involve a full cure to disease. Sometimes it involves remission, endurance, even acceptance of death while trusting in the ultimate healing and hope found in the risen triumphant Lord. Jesus promises nothing less than eternal life, empowered courage, and constant companionship. May you realize that God is at work to encourage you and give you hope. May our humanity be sanctified through the blessings that are born out of suffering and hope. Soul fruit is born from struggle when faith is rooted in God, our Creator and Redeemer.

2. Finding God at Work in Your Soul
(A diagnosis and the blessing of faith)

On a day in late November, 2002, the weather was partly sunny with a slight chill as I drove to see our family doctor for a follow-up visit from some blood tests. Little did I know that God was at work to "bless" my soul that day with the truth about my condition of health. The information I was given would require an increase of faith and reliance upon God, and faith in those who He would lead me to trust. The main symptoms were: constant fatigue, pain in my lower left front side, breaking into cold sweats at night, and becoming short of breath after climbing just one flight of stairs. So there I was, sitting alone quietly in patient room number three, starring at posters of the skeletal system and thinking of how incredible God had made us. Dr. Orlando Benedict came in and opened my chart. After a few pleasant greetings he looked down to see the results of my recent blood tests. He spoke softly to himself as he reread the findings. He then said, "It looks as though your blood levels are very low. In fact, I am very concerned." His eyes widened as he looked at me. "I want you to see a good friend of mine, a hematologist, Dr. Danish." In that moment I was partly in shock, and also quite aware of the potential danger I might be facing. My brother had died of cancer at age 40, and now here I was at age 44 wondering if history was repeating itself. "Do I have cancer?" I asked. He mentioned it was too soon to say, but then acknowledged, "You very well may have cancer." I told him that I was not afraid, and that God would help me through whatever I would go through. Beyond the initial shock, this was my hopeful response. But I did not know the severity of the situation, so why not be optimistic?

Being a Christian himself, Dr. Benedict affirmed the healing work of God. He stepped out of the room, made a quick phone call, and convinced Dr. Danish to see me within a few hours. Meanwhile, I sat quietly on the examining table and prayed: "Jesus I trust that you will help me." I sensed that the Lord was near and that I was not alone. I believed in my soul that God would provide the help I needed. Dr. Benedict returned with my appointment being set that afternoon as he gave me the address to Dr. Danish's office. I walked out to my car somewhat stunned with the possibility that I probably had cancer. Many things ran through my mind, but most of all there was that initial shock, and the question: "Is this really happening?" Grasping the gravity of what was going on was gradual that day, and my feelings were about as definable as shattered glass.

I started the car and began to drive to the First Baptist Church of Grand Blanc, Michigan where I was pastor. I called my wife Marilyn at the hospital where she worked as a nurse. When I told her what my blood levels were she became alarmed. Her voice became strained and strong. "What are you doing driving and talking with me on the phone with blood like that?" She went on: "Where are you right now?" "Near the church, a few blocks away", I replied trying to remain calm as I was driving. "Don't do anything until I can come and go with you to Dr. Danish."

I arrived at church and waited quietly in my office. I prayed and wondered what would happen next. I realized my life was going to change, but in what way? I told our church secretary, Mary Ann, and she initiated the prayer chain. The wheels were in motion for support and prayer. Marilyn had now been released by her supervisor at Genesys Hospital; she came immediately to pick me up at the church and then proceeded to bring me to Dr. Danish's office. We sat there in the busy clinic holding hands, wondering what was going to happen in our lives through this experience. She explained that the blood levels I had were very dangerous, especially my low platelet count. "If you get in an accident they will not be able to easily stop the bleeding." I didn't realize how sick I had become. I just thought I had been out of shape. I was glad I had talked with my doctor and he had the wisdom to order blood tests. Now here I was, hoping that this detour in our lives would not be too difficult or devastating. I took comfort in the peace that Christ had given to my heart since I had come to know Him as a young man. Still, I began to think of how this fight with cancer was going to affect my wife and three sons.

In the midst of the busy doctor's clinic my mind wandered back in time, I remembered how my brother Bruce had battled kidney cancer for eight years before he couldn't fight it anymore. Now, here I was, sitting in a cancer clinic. I remembered how he grew in his faith, how he was courageous, how he gained strength for a while and found blessings in the midst of his difficult battle with cancer. I was now beginning to brace myself and adjust my thoughts and schedule toward whatever lay ahead. "Scott Arnold" the receptionist called out. On our way to the examining room a stretcher was being wheeled out with a patient on route for the hospital. The cancer treatments had left him bald and weak. My heart was moved with this man's struggle, yet inwardly I wondered if I had just looked into a mirror of my future. I began to realize that I was entering a new chapter of life.

The nurse came in to the patient room and asked me many questions. Dr. Danish soon came in and looked at me and then my chart and exclaimed pointedly: "What's the matter with you? You're blood levels are very low and you don't look well." "Do I have cancer?" I asked. "You very well might" he said, "the first thing we must do is have a bone marrow biopsy tomorrow morning and then a blood transfusion immediately afterward." "What is the likelihood that I have cancer?" I asked. "Very likely", he said, "and very possibly Leukemia or Lymphoma." He noted that my spleen had become enlarged and that this was because my bone marrow had not been producing enough

15

healthy blood cells and my spleen had become a holding place for all my unhealthy blood cells. He explained that if I had cancer in my bone marrow it would prohibit the production of good cells and hence make me feel tired. He further cautioned me about doing anything risky that could initiate internal or external bleeding. Though he considered having me admitted into the hospital, he allowed me to go home and prepare for the biopsy and transfusion. Knowing my wife was a nurse gave him assurance that I would be closely cared for.

The two of us walked out of the office with a sense of heaviness, and a concern that moved us to greater prayer and closer care for one another and our children. Marilyn drove me home as we awaited the beginning of a journey that called for deepened faith in the Lord's power to heal. Still, we did not know what kind of cancer I had. The most important thing then was to take each day as it came, and seek God's strength and provision of help. The realization of how seriously low my blood levels had become did not hit me until I looked closely in the mirror and saw how pale my face and complexion were. Furthermore, I noticed how my strength was shaky and my breathing was shallow as I moved about with simple exercise. I had not been listening carefully to what my body was telling me, and I could no longer just assume a "tough guy" attitude would solve my problems.

Earlier in the day, Mark (a senior in High School) had picked up Thom (8th grade) and John (5th grade) from their schools. By the time we had arrived home from the doctor's office our sons were aware and were at home waiting with concern. That evening we talked and prayed together about my health crisis.

As the sun was setting, and it was becoming dark, we sat down in the living room and told them about the blood tests and of the possibility of cancer. I could see that they were struggling to understand what all this meant; their non-verbal response included sadly putting their face into the sofa or into their hands. There were tears of concern from each one; Marilyn and I openly expressed our feelings too. We confessed our concerns and yet held on to faith. Later, while seated around the dinner table, I led my family in prayer. We desperately needed God's help. I explained that while I was honestly afraid, I trusted that God would answer our prayers as we placed our faith completely in the Lord. Our sons did not know what to say or think. This was understandable in that they had little experience with knowing someone who had cancer. We expressed to them that this was serious, and that we would need them to work together to take up some of my responsibilities. Their anxiety increased with eyes that were wide open, wondering what all this meant. There was not much more we could prepare them for, especially since there were still many unknowns. With this we prayed, and we felt God's comforting presence in the midst of uncertainty. The experience of waiting upon God was bearing (in time) the fruit of reliance and faith.

We contacted family and church members and a broader prayer chain was activated. I heard my wife talking on the cell phone, and I realized that a call was going out to a great host of people to pray for me. This support of intercession was a humbling experience, deep within I felt encouraged. In time we would hear of people in just about every continent, and throughout many churches in our city, state, and around the nation who joined us in prayer.

God used this crisis to move the hearts of many people to pray. However, there was nothing quite as sweet to my soul as the prayers of my wife, children, parents, and close family and friends. Their prayers lifted me up in hope and warmed my heart with joy. All these prayers went up to God as a fragrant offering. There were many steps toward healing, but the first priority for us was faith and prayer in God's presence and intervention. God would answer personally and powerfully.

The doctor's office was quiet the next morning at 8 a.m. as Marilyn and I arrived. Dr. Danish and his assistant Sandy were ready to perform the bone marrow biopsy. He was in a jovial mood, less stressed than the previous day. He explained that the biopsy would hurt but that it would heal up in a week or so. As I lay on the table he said: "Now this will be a piece of cake! No. A piece of Danish!" Then, with local anesthesia applied, he extracted the bone marrow (in corkscrew manner mind you) from my hip bone. Yes it did hurt, but I would rather have pain to remind me of being alive than to have no pain and no life. He then said that it would take at least several weeks to know the results. This seemed like a long time, but then again this was the first time I had been through anything like this. I asked him "Why so long?" He explained that they had to ship the specimens to several labs, one in Texas and the other in Georgia. These pathologists in separate labs would then go through an elaborate process of finding the cells and determining what type of cancer it is. "We will schedule an ultrasound and colonoscopy this week, and a CT-Scan within a few weeks." "Now what am supposed to do?", I asked. "You will have to make changes and take precautions to avoid becoming infected; your white blood cell count is too low. You will have to modify the way you interact with people." "What do you mean?" I wondered. He pointed at my hand: "You can't shake hands or hug. You can't go visit people in hospitals or nursing homes. You must use hand sanitizers and avoid public places. You can't eat most fresh fruit or fresh vegetables. You must avoid any dangerous activity where you would get bruised or cut."

In that moment it hit me, this would be a challenge, particularly in my calling as a pastor. What would I do on Sunday mornings? Would I walk around with body guards, rubber gloves, a mask, and a bubble shield? "What about my visitation responsibilities?" I asked him. He just looked at me and said, "You must delegate these responsibilities."

At that time I knew that I had to clarify concerns with the leaders of the church and come up with a strategy. When I asked the doctor how long it would take for a more specific diagnosis he told me it may take several weeks.

The next stop that morning was the infusion clinic. It was a long room with about ten beds. There were three other patients there getting started with blood transfusions. The nurses worked carefully to make sure that each of us received the right match of blood, and that we were receiving the blood at the proper rate. Several of the other patients had lost their hair as they were in the midst of treatments to fight Leukemia. I wondered if I too had Leukemia. I tried to relax and make myself at home; but I was still in a mindset of being active. So I brought my laptop and was planning on doing some work or reading a book. The reality of being sick was still setting in, and yet I was still planning on preaching that Sunday. The infusion nurse came up to me and encouraged me to relax as she found my vein and began preparing me. It would take about 6-8 hours to give me several units of blood.

During this time we were blessed to have our friend Dr. Wendy Balivet from the church stop by. She brought a miniature "Boggle" word game and an entertaining book for reading. The blessing of friends showing thoughtfulness was moving my heart to a depth of unexpected appreciation. I was not accustomed to being the one ministered to, the one on the receiving end. The support and care of friends, family, and church began to increase. To this day I am humbled and grateful for the great compassion people are capable of as God inspires them. We discovered the curative power of kindness. Caring souls had touched us deeply, even more than we could have imagined, as we were in a situation of great need.

With the blood transfusion, it turned out that the nurse who helped us was Filipino, as is Marilyn, and they had common experiences culturally and professionally. In every respect through that day I was blessed with people being present. The gift of blood was helping me that day because of someone's unselfish sacrifice. I thought of my Savior Jesus who gave His life blood for me on the cross. I reaffirmed my faith in Jesus, His closeness, and the vital power of God's Spirit at work within me. Jesus' blood was shed to forgive my sins. Furthermore, His lifeblood was at work in my soul's "spiritual veins" as well. Whatever would happen, I found peace in the knowledge of God's grace and my Savior's healing power.

When I did go in to have the ultrasound several days later, the doctors confirmed the existence of tumors, but not much more detail than that. The colonoscopy scheduled that day was cancelled, which was fine by me because someone at the waiting room commented sarcastically: "You haven't lived until you've had a colonoscopy, it's awful." I noticed then, and at a few other times, how patients can be very negative when they are struggling with the unknown and the unpleasant. In a way, the expression of anger and sarcasm gives people a temporary sense of staying on top of their problems. Instead, we would all be better served to find true lasting peace to deal with life's pains and problems.

The leaders of the church I served were supportive during this time. However, many people unaware of how those with cancer have compromised immune systems. The first two Sundays after my initial diagnosis and infusion there were many people who wanted a handshake or a hug. Restraint was difficult. All of us were having a hard time making the transition. I made sure, however, to use plenty of hand sanitizer between contacts. Dry skin was a reasonable compromise, but I realized then how much we all rely upon touch to communicate care and concern. Not until you are told to avoid contact with people do you realize that touch is a deep and profound expression of love and support. Touch is such a vital part of our human communication, that to live without it challenges one's sense of connection and wholeness.

The days went by slowly before the CT-Scan and my next doctor's office visit. My doctor had since moved into a new facility and I would go there weekly for blood tests. Within another week I needed another infusion, including platelets. I was growing increasingly aware of the seriousness of my condition. While I continued to work at church, attend meetings, lead worship, preach, contact people by phone, accept appointments at the office, and write for the church newsletter; I was still restricted. The sacrifice was that I could not go to many public places. I must say that I didn't like these limitations. However, the Christmas season was upon us. The joy and expression of God's peace brought us through the gloom of wondering what would happen or of thinking pessimistically. The message was clear: Jesus is our "Emmanuel", "God with us." We grew in faith once again celebrating the blessing of Jesus and His nativity. The reality of God's incarnation increased in its significant. Carols such as "Hark the Herald Angels Sing" and "Silent Night" became fresh and meaningful. We were more aware of the need for "peace on earth and mercy mild" and one who made it possible for God and sinners to be "reconciled." In the silent moments of Christmas I would feel the presence of my Lord encouraging reverence and deepening faith. In the silence of preparation on Christmas Eve I looked at the gifts and stockings and wondered if this would be my last Christmas. I took comfort to know that God was in control and we are His children through faith in a Savior who was born in Bethlehem. I felt His loving presence in my heart and that was enough, the precious gift that I needed. The joy and warmth of care that we shared that day transcended gift-giving; we were a family of faith trusting in Jesus.

After Christmas, the day soon came for the CT-Scan. I drank the contrast, a strange citrus flavored shake, then dressed in a meager light blue gown, went into the CT-Scan room, laid down on my back on a sliding table, was given intravenous dye, and was then scanned by a machine that revolved around me while making whirling sounds. A robotic voice commanded me when to breath in and out, hold my breath, or be still. Though I was both anxious and fascinated, I have since found these tests to be fun. The question still concerned us: What would they find? Marilyn was watching, and went to the radiologist's room. The radiologist, a Frenchman, was reading the scans as I had now redressed and joined Marilyn down the hallway at the CT-Scan reading room. Normally it takes a day or so to find out the results. However, this radiologist kindly motioned us in and showed us where my cancer was and how large my spleen was. I watched as he turned a dial that showed various cross sections of my body. Each section showed the width of various organs, bones, and tumors. There were five tumors, a few of them as large as tangerines, throughout my abdomen. He indicated that they were in the location of my lymph nodes. He indicated that this was a good sign, for Lymphoma was easier to treat than Leukemia. He then indicated that I was in stage four with my cancer. I asked him what "stage four" meant. "Stage four is the last stage of cancer before you die," he said. "It has moved from your lymph nodes and has entered your bone marrow." The doctor's words startled me. The scans made it clear that this was not something that had been caught in the early stages. A silence of wonderment and awe swept over me, as I found God's peace and serenity for the moment. The radiologist then added, "if you are going to have any type of advanced cancer, this type is one that can be treated with hope." In my heart I knew that Christ was with me. My wife and I realized that this was a serious situation, but there was hope. At least I was not facing a cancer that would be impossible to treat. The next morning I would see Dr. Danish.

The doctor's office was busy at 7:30am that day. I looked at the wide assortment of people and realized how many people of various ages, races, and economic situations have cancer. I saw those who looked weak and frail and those who had strength and vitality. I saw those who had peace and those who were anxious and fearful. Here I was, still inwardly adjusting to being a "cancer patient", waiting to find out officially from Dr. Danish exactly what my diagnosis of cancer was. Would it be hopeful or dreadful? Would I have a long life to look forward to, or was this a time when I would find out that I was only going to live a few months or years longer? We went in to the examining room. He came in the room and looked at the charts, the results of an ultra sound, the results of the CT scan, and was looking for the bone marrow biopsy reports. Seeing that the biopsy reports were not too specific, he went out and set up a conference call with the two labs. Then he came back and reported that their best guess was that I had a type of Non- Hodgkin's Lymphoma. He then said that there are many types of Non Hodgkin's Lymphoma, some fast and others slow in their growth. In his conference call their hypothesis was that mine was a medium to slow growing type. He told us that it could be treated with Chemotherapy and Immunotherapy, but he was still concerned about how enlarged my spleen was. For a moment he debated whether or not to recommend the surgical removal of the spleen. But then he said "we need to focus on fighting the cancer first." He asked me how I was doing. By this time he was aware of my being a Christian minister, and he said: "People of faith typically do better than people who don't have faith." I wasn't sure what his faith was, but I was encouraged to hear him say this. I responded, "I trust in Jesus Christ; He is with us."

Dr. Danish laid out the plan for treatment. I would need a few more blood transfusions before having a simple surgery to receive my "mediport" for the treatments. The chemotherapy would begin the second week of January. Lingering unanswerable questions abounded. What struggles lay ahead of us? Would the chemotherapy work? What about my family and their emotional state? What about my calling and responsibilities as a pastor? What about finances? Would I loose my hair? How would the steroids affect me? How difficult would this battle be? There were more questions than answers, and when that happens we must trust God to straighten out life's question marks so that in time they become faith exclamation marks!!! Our faith is sometimes all we have to go on, and yet in truth we walk more by faith than sight than we often care to admit.

The choice is ours whether or not to receive the support of God's Son and Holy Spirit when we go through faith-stretching experiences. Some will doubt and deny the nearness of Jesus or dismiss His Lordship over their lives. I believe, however, that we must ultimately trust our Heavenly Father, His Son Jesus as the Great Physician. I believe there is great power at work when we surrender in faith to trust God in prayer. In those early days of dealing with cancer our world was shaken in order to rely upon the foundation of our faith in God, and that was a blessing. The shake-up that all cancer patients experience will either make or break one's resolve, character, and faith. I was determined to see how this battle could refine my character. I was already beginning to experience the fruit of God's Spirit working in my soul. Nevertheless, I was also bracing myself to endure a number of rounds of therapy and other unknown challenges.

Soon after the doctor's specific diagnosis in early January of 2003, I met with church leaders to share with them the specifics and extent of immediate and ongoing treatments. I relayed to them that, according to Dr. Danish, I would have some initial good results in six months if my body responded well. Meanwhile, I had resolved to continue preaching and was scheduled to baptize several people the Sunday before I would start Chemotherapy. About a week before the treatments began, a group of men from the church came to our home. Together we had a meaningful time of prayer where at one point they anointed my head with oil as an expression of faith in God's healing touch. The scripture that God gave to us at that time was from Paul's letter to the Hebrews.

Therefore, since we are surrounded by such a great cloud of witnesses, let us throw off everything that hinders and the sin that so easily entangles, and let us run with perseverance the race marked out for us. ² Let us fix our eyes on Jesus, the author and perfecter of our faith, who for the joy set before him endured the cross, scorning its shame, and sat down at the right hand of the throne of God. (Hebrews 12:1-2 NIV)

This time of prayer was a beautiful affirmation of brotherly affection. I was at peace in being emotionally and spiritually prepared, positioned in the blessing of being surrounded by a great "cloud of witnesses". I think of a "cloud" of witnesses as being like a "crowd" that includes both those living on earth and those who are in heaven. Being a part of God's community of believers is one of the most important blessings to cherish in life. God was teaching me to be more appreciative and understanding of others in various situations of illness, struggle, or suffering. God was broadening the scope of my empathy and compassion. God was teaching our whole family the meaning and reality of sufficient grace. The Apostle Paul had once commented about his own "thorn in the flesh":

Three times I pleaded with the Lord to take it away from me. But he said to me, "My grace is sufficient for you, for my power is made perfect in weakness." Therefore I will boast all the more gladly about my weaknesses, so that Christ's power may rest on me. That is why, for Christ's sake, I delight in weaknesses, in insults, in hardships, in persecutions, in difficulties. For when I am weak, then I am strong. (2 Corinthians 12:8-10 NIV)

The Apostle Paul's conclusion was that he had been given illness for a purpose. There was blessing in his

25

weakness, there lessons to learn while dealing with a thorn in his flesh that would not go away. Even with this continuing struggle Paul could testify that God's grace is always sufficient. In hopeful expectation, Paul even delighted in what God could do to shine through his illness. Liabilities can be transformed into assets. Character does arise from suffering. Outside sources of strength are discovered when one accepts their own weaknesses. Indeed, Christ's power was the hope that we rested upon in those days. God was at work pruning and preparing us to bear the fruit of faith.

A picture Thom took of Scott in a car mirror.

3. The Intervention of God
(Cancer Treatment and Faith at Work)

A few snow flakes whisked around the car as we came up to the Genesys/Hurley Cancer Institute in Flint, Michigan. Marilyn and I went in through the welcome center and then up the slow moving elevator. As the doors opened to a large waiting room and lobby, we were instructed to go left to the entrance of a nice new "chemo" clinic. The nurses were expecting me, even though they were busy as I signed in. The place was full and buzzing between those who were there for chemotherapy, people having their blood tested, people receiving shots of white blood cell booster ("Neupogen"), and those who were there with their loved ones for support. The nurses moved quickly with smiles and humor, and it became clear that they had developed a strong sense of teamwork. The first step was to take a small vial of my blood, and then the nurse put it in a special machine that analyzed my blood cells and give us the results in just a few minutes. Nothing had improved greatly from my infusions; all my blood count levels were still very low. I wondered how I would do with chemotherapy. The nurse brought us into a room where we watched a video about how the treatment worked and gave information about what to expect. I was very calm, I wondered if I was perhaps even too relaxed about all of this.

After a short while I was seated in a recliner where I would be given my first chemotherapy. The nurse put a needle into my mediport and prepared a line for treatment. She hooked up a bottle on an I.V. stand with a blue liquid called "Mitoxantrone "; I called it "Smurf juice" (after the blue cartoon characters). It works by blocking an enzyme involved with cell division so that existing cancer cells don't continue to divide into new cells. After this, I was given a drip of "Benadryl" to prepare me for the upcoming immunotherapy called "Rituxin." This is a monoclonal antibody prepared in the laboratory that is made to identify and attach to the cancer cells. Once it attaches to the cancer cells the body's white blood cells come along and kill the cancer cells. The trick is, however, that when it first enters your body it is seen as an intruder and is attacked by the bloodstream's antibodies. Some people are able to receive it without too much difficulty, but others are not as able to receive it because their body rejects it. The nurse told me that they would introduce it slowly at first and see how I would react. The first ten minutes were fine, but then I started to feel jittery, very soon I began to shiver and shake, breaking out into a cold sweat. It was scary and something I could not simply "tough out". My body's immune system was counteracting this intrusion. The nurse stopped the treatment. By this time it was too late to continue anymore for the day, we would have to try again tomorrow. This was not the result that we had hoped for.

The next morning the nurse repeated the procedures and informed me that it was important to get more of the Rituxan (Rituximab) into my system. My body needed to treat these new antibodies as a friend and not as a foe. I wondered why the person next to me in the treatment room the previous day did not have any difficulties with receiving their first round. So this time I decided to take a different mental and spiritual approach. The previous day I tried to be quiet and still, peaceful and serene. This time I came in expecting this to be "a battle". I was ready and prepared in prayer for a fight. When the antibodies were being introduced I was upright, not lying down. I made it point to talk more with Marilyn and others during the treatment. I brought my Bible so that I could fight with the power of God's word. I brought a good book entitled "People Sharing Jesus" by Darrell Robinson. Our church was about to use this with a theme on evangelism, starting that upcoming Sunday. I also brought a cell phone. Why did I bring my cell phone? I needed to call a guest preacher and friend regarding the church revival services that were being planned several weeks from then. In the midst of this treatment I found that it helped me to be engaged in some form of planning for the future. I learned that by doing what is of utmost importance, what our calling is, we are given perspective and strength to overcome whatever challenges may press upon us. In this critical time I needed to be engaged, not detached, from the spiritual battle that was underneath the physical battle with cancer. While I had passively relied upon the grace and power of God in the first day of treatment, this time I was better prepared through mental and spiritual alertness. In reflection I wrote my observations down for my sermon manuscript on January 19, 2003:

I must tell you that in the midst of my struggle this week with Chemotherapy, I learned a few lessons. First, be alert in the spiritual battle; don't rest too comfortably in God's grace. The most difficult part of Chemotherapy so far came when my body had to accept the strong antibody treatment of Rituxan. Would my body accept it? The first day I received the treatment I reclined in the chair as my body soon reacted by chills and shaking. They had to stop. The next day they hoped for a better result, and I did better, sitting up alert and ready as they gave me the treatment. The third day they increased the speed of drip, as I had needed to receive much more. When I was reclined again I once again reacted, this time with hives and an allergic reaction. Not quite giving up, they gave me Benedryl, then tried again, this time I was up and alert, ready for a fight, putting my mind and body in a battle mode. With God's help I was able to take the remaining dose of the Chemo medication. This antibody treatment was going directly into my bloodstream to my bone marrow and cancer cells in my lymph nodes and throughout my body. The battle was indeed on.

A second lesson that I learned from this was that God's grace is not to be seen always as a matter of rest, sometimes the grace of God is difficult, calling for alertness for the battles we face. When I reclined back in the chair, my body did not do as well with the chemo, but when I was alert and ready, I was able to win the battle.

Sometimes as Christians we are too comfortable in the grace of God. That is when we loose ground in life's battles because we do not stay alert and ready. We must resist the devil, and go through sufferings. God himself will restore us and make us strong as we remain FIRM and STEADFAST.

A passage of scripture that helped me during those three days of battling the reaction to the Immunotherapy came from Peter's letter to the church in the midst of their struggles:

Humble yourselves, therefore, under God's mighty hand, that he may lift you up in due time. Cast all your anxiety on him because he cares for you. Be self-controlled and alert. Your enemy the devil prowls around like a roaring lion looking for someone to devour. Resist him, standing firm in the faith, because you know that your brothers throughout the world are undergoing the same kind of sufferings. And the God of all grace, who called you to his eternal glory in Christ, after you have suffered a little while, will himself restore you and make you strong, firm and steadfast. To him be the power for ever and ever. Amen. (I Peter 5:6-11)

The word of action here is to "resist" the enemy in order to stand firm in the faith. I literally stayed at the edge of my chair and prayed hard to overcome this mountain.

By the time the week of treatment was over, I had overcome a large hurdle; my body had accepted the Rituxin antibodies as a friendly force for good. The parallel to how people react to God, or Jesus Christ and the Holy Spirit can be drawn. Though the intervention of God is good for us, and can cleanse us from sin, and help us win the battle with destructive cancer in our soul; there are many who resist God and reject the truth that could set them free. The reality of our need for a work of tough grace means accepting the battle, not simply sitting back and thinking that we have no part in God's work of salvation. Our part is faith and courage, not shrinking back when the going gets tough, but staying strong in hope and obedience. The surrender that we must embrace is to cling to the promises, presence, and power of God. When we willingly accept the truth of the gospel of Jesus Christ we are promised victory over sin and death. We experience the working of God through faith, and faith is the hopeful surrender of a trusting soul. But faith will be tested, and there will be a fight for our souls. However, we can overcome with the help of Christ Jesus, our Savior King, who enables us to resist the devil and refrain from evil. When we are obedient to God it will mean resistance to evil.

In this initial battle I had learned the value of tough grace. Humbling ourselves is not a passive thing. Faith and determination is needed to put away the attitudes, behaviors, and emotions that can keep us from fulfilling God's will for our lives. Waiting for the moving of God takes prayer and trust, something that can not be rushed. Waiting for the healing of God involves "casting" our cares on Him and believing He will carry us over the "troubled waters". For those who battle cancer, and for those who are helping a loved one battle cancer, God guides us to acknowledge and release our burdens, fears, and anxiety. We must trust in God's loving care, for this will help us to be self-controlled and alert as we are tested and will go through trials. In fact, in the midst of fighting cancer physically one discovers that cancer involves a spiritual battle as well. The disciple Peter observed that Satan prowls around like a devouring lion. If fear grips us we are going to be consumed, eaten alive! What are we to do about this? Resist Him! What are we to do about cancer?

31

Resist it! Humble yourselves before God, and wait upon His presence and power. In Jesus name resist cancer. Understand that many others are going through the same kind of sufferings, even though each situation is unique. Trust in God's grace; suffer a little while with the hope of restoration. God has the power to heal. If that healing is given directly in our life upon earth, or if that healing is to prepare our souls for heaven, either way God is to be praised and glorified. Yes, God may even be praised and glorified through fighting cancer. This is a tremendous blessing, an experience that many people have shared. Cancer is not the end, but a new chapter with a direction that requires vulnerability, faith, and reliance.

Reliance upon God leads us to place great hope in God's promises. Isaiah was a prophet who led God's people through catastrophic trials. His resilient faith was inspiring because he had come to trust in the Lord and wait upon His strength for the healing and deliverance of the nation of Israel. Though the people had struggled with their own internal sins, which can affect a nation much like cancer, they also were being threatened from the outside by Babylon and other nations. Being overwhelmed by the spread of several aggressive civilizations that wanted to overrun them, they needed God's help to overcome, survive, and even thrive. The word of the Lord came to Isaiah as he spoke God's hope into their lives:

Why do you say, O Jacob, and complain, O Israel, "My way is hidden from the LORD; my cause is disregarded by my God"? Do you not know? Have you not heard? The LORD is the everlasting God, the Creator of the ends of the earth. He will not grow tired or weary, and his understanding no one can fathom. He gives strength to the weary and increases the power of the weak. Even youths grow tired and weary, and young men stumble and fall; but those who hope in the LORD will renew their strength. They will soar on wings like eagles; they will run and not grow weary, they will walk and not be faint. (Isaiah 40:27-31)

Do you see the connection in the preceding passage to the battle with cancer or other types of illness? Like the Hebrew patriarchs Jacob or Job we wrestle or argue with God on the level of why difficult things happen in life. Like the nation of Israel we complain to God about our problems instead of realizing that nothing is hidden from God. We think that God does not regard our cancer or is not interested in our "little" lives. In self pity we despair our outcome, and we look at the grave instead of the skies. We minimize God's strength and mercy, and we lack faith in the promise of His everlasting covenant. Sometimes we even project our own limitation upon the Lord, as if He has grown tired or can't understand. In fact, God is in control and the battle with cancer or any other disease can bring us to a greater faith, a greater love for the Lord, and a greater compassion for others.

In the midst of the journey, God gives us strength when we grow weary. God intervenes for the weak with power from His throne of grace. Young and old alike may be attacked by cancer, and be humbled and weakened. Yet there is one common hope: *"Those who hope in the Lord will renew their strength."* The images of soaring like eagles, running with endurance like an Olympic athlete, or at least being able to walk through life's garden with strength enough to enjoy a slower pace, all speak hope to us of God's restoring power. These three images also help us to have the right balance of perspective. God helps us soar to see things from above, the bigger picture. God helps us to run so as to joyfully spread the good news of His grace and truth in Jesus Christ to others. God helps us to walk to see things close up and personal, to have intimate communion with us. In life we need all three of these dimensions: vision, purpose, and intimacy. This has direct application to the battle with cancer. God wants us to be blessed and bear fruit at every level by being renewed through His vision, His purpose, and His intimacy. God will work through people, and likewise God will also intervene personally as the one who renews our strength in every aspect of life.

I am reminded of a miracle that happened some time after my oldest brother Bruce's death from Renal (Kidney) cancer. My mother was driving along a road near my home town of Midland, Michigan. She was returning from a shopping mall where she had purchased a ceramic eagle with Isaiah 40:31 inscribed on it. She had bought it as a reminder of God's promises in the midst of her grief of losing her firstborn son just months earlier. Much to her surprise and amazement a large bird swooped and soared into her view on Tittabawasee River road. She looked carefully and observed the white head and broad brown wings. She immediately called my father and told him all about it. He was at work at the Midland Foundation and acknowledged what she saw but indicated that it was not likely an eagle. Eagles in that part of the state had not been seen in many decades. Right after their conversation he received a call from someone who worked in the county building in downtown Midland. In the midst of their dialogue the man interrupted, "I can't believe what I am seeing out my window. There's a bald eagle flying around." To this day we believe God sent the eagle as a sign of grace and hope. Years before, our family had adopted the eagle as a symbol because the name "Arnold" means "as strong as an eagle." We even put an eagle decal on our aluminum canoe. God used the eagle that day as a way of revealing divine hope and promise for *"those who wait upon Him shall rise up with wings like eagles"*.

After this first round of Chemotherapy and Immunotherapy, I remembered how Dr. Danish had told me that people who have faith do better with battling cancer. I had told him that I appreciated him as a good doctor, but that I was also trusting in Jesus Christ as my "Great Physician". Dr. Danish smiled as he appeared to be wondering about what made this Christian minister "tick". Throughout this time God encouraged me through the following words of promise: *Let us draw near to God with a sincere heart in full assurance of faith, having our hearts sprinkled to cleanse us from a guilty conscience and having our bodies washed with pure water. Let us hold unswervingly to the hope we profess, for he who promised is faithful.* (Hebrews 10:22-23)

Though the chemotherapy would kill many of my body's cells, both good and bad, I held on to the hope that I had known in Christ. Even though there would be delayed side effects to the treatments, and I knew that it would be difficult at times, it did not make me depressed. Instead, the experience of going through cancer brought me closer to God. I trusted in the faithfulness of God to cleanse me, remake me, and even grant a new heart within me. I found peace in the knowledge that He faithfully held me in the palm of His hand. In the midst of accepting my mortality, the immortal grasp of God's love gently held me firm. I felt as though my soul had drawn near to God, and this proximity was bearing fruit through the springs of living water that Jesus gave within my innermost parts.

Bless the LORD, O my soul: and all that is within me, bless his holy name. Bless the LORD, O my soul, and forget not all his benefits: Who forgiveth all thine iniquities; who healeth all thy diseases; Who redeemeth thy life from destruction; who crowneth thee with loving kindness and tender mercies; Who satisfieth thy mouth with good things; so that thy youth is renewed like the eagle's.

Psalms 103:1-5 (KJV)

4. The Power of an Encounter with God
(Worship, prayer, and praise)

The effect of the chemotherapy started to hit me as I felt weakness throughout my body and weariness in my soul. There is a weird uneasy feeling that comes when your body is trying to cope with chemicals or antibodies that it has never dealt with before. To describe what it feels like is like trying to explain a twitchy feeling that pulls at your emotions while your body lacks rest and comfort for days on end. Energy levels vacillate like the ocean tide. Each person I talked with at the clinic had somewhat different experiences, but the common threads of struggle that wove us together were discomfort, tiredness, sacrifice, being overwhelmed, and most of all having concern for our families. For those who had faith in God's presence and power at the clinic there were common threads of hope, peace, love, and prayers. We shared a greater reliance upon God that wove us together as a community blessed by the working of God's grace.

As expected, the chemo affected my appetite. At first I was not very hungry, but then I noticed that the steroids they put me on made me crave certain things. I woke up one morning and started to cook eggs at 4:00a.m. Sardines were also appealing to me as I began to surmise my interest was in salty things to eat. I did crave fresh fruits and vegetables, but these were forbidden, unless they had a cover, like bananas or oranges. For some patients, food is a challenge and they lose weight during chemotherapy. One of my doctors, Dr. Kang who put in my mediport, advised that I should try to eat well during treatment. I took his advice and in time did find there were things that I could eat that did not make me nauseous. The key concern about appetite was that I needed nutrition for strength in the battle with cancer. One thing that I did not anticipate was the need for water, and lots of it. This was essential, because dehydration can hit you quickly and take you down fast. In the midst of eating and doing all the right things for treatment, I made sure that I did not neglect my spiritual sustenance. Prayer was a vital part of every day, every hour, and many profound minutes and seconds.

I was experiencing a closer walk with Christ and an awareness of His mercy and grace that deepened. In prayer I felt more and more caught up in the Spirit. There was peace that flowed into my soul as I opened up my heart to God. The words of Scripture stabilized my soul as the bedrock of my being. In this time of physical weakness I concentrated on where my strength lay, with the Lord, the maker and redeemer of my life. My heart would lift up praise to God, and the silent song of my soul began to shine strongly within. I worshipped God in the quiet beauty of solitude. Each morning and night, and early afternoon, I would make time for worship. In fact, my belief that all of life is to be worshipful unto God intensified. Worshipful living is full and rich, a way of life that can even see the role of pain, suffering, persecution, grief, yes even cancer, in the whole movement of God's sufficient grace and triumphant glory. This battle with cancer had now taken on a significance that I had not imagined or expected. I sought to discover the redeeming value of fighting cancer. God's very presence led me to understand that my life's current battle called for a deeper faith, a closer walk with Jesus. Life's worshipful essence grew as I accepted my body's mortality and embraced my spirit's immortality in connection with Christ my risen Lord and Savior. Going through this time of trust and obedience had a way of refining my faith into its basic elements. Suffering allowed me to be reshaped and remade as I trusted God, believing in His wondrous love and healing power.

One night, about a week after I had finished my first treatment, I had an encounter with my Lord and Savior Jesus Christ that changed my life. I was upright in bed, reading scripture and praying. Marilyn had fallen asleep, and I was wide awake as I continued in prayer, praise, and meditation. For at least twenty minutes I had enjoyed a time of singing within my heart. With my mouth moving from a desire to bless the Lord, I silently breathed out the words of praise. I sensed within this time of worship that I was before God's throne of grace. I had begun this time of worship with reading scripture, I then asked God for understanding regarding my cancer and His plan for my life. I poured out my concerns before my Savior and Lord Jesus, surrendering all these concerns as I entered this time of worship. With this prayerful release I began to move more into the aspect of my adoration of God. I began to give praise to His might and mercy, His truth and righteousness, His awe and majesty, His glory and grace. As my praise moved more away from my problems to the power and presence of God, peace and joy grew within my soul. I felt that I had entered the holy of holies, His presence was near. I had prayed in this way before, and had experienced the power of God's Holy Spirit that comforts, counsels, and blesses us when we deeply pray in God's presence. But this time something else was about to happen that I will never forget.

In the midst of praising God, and my Lord and Savior Jesus Christ, I sensed a brightness filling and transforming the bedroom. The brightness became intense. If you can imagine the most pure, clean, light possible it would still pale in comparison to the radiance and splendor of the light that filled the room. In the midst of this glorious brightness I could make out a figure from whom the brightness was coming from. Without a doubt I knew it was Jesus. He came to me and began to place His hands upon me. This was all so intense and powerful that at first I began to cry in joy and hope. I was speechless and filled with awe and love. When His hands touched my shoulders and head there was a power that swept through my body. I felt that there was healing in my body, a great peace permeated my soul, as I continued to worship Jesus Christ my Lord and Savior, and give glory to God my Heavenly Father. His brightness remained for a few minutes and then faded away. The joy of my heart did not fade away. My lips could not speak at first, but my soul sang ever so finely in the remaining glow of God's grace bestowed by His Son Jesus, the one who is the Lamb of God, worthy of all honor and praise. This moment of grace given by the Son of God has been remembered every day since. My vision ever since is that He is with me, ever so near, my Savior and friend who is the Great Physician, the Good Shepherd of my soul.

In that moment of grace outpoured, the Lord had revealed Himself to me and had touched me with healing power. I wanted to tell my wife, but I was speechless for at least 30-40 minutes. Somehow, when you are in the presence of God, time is hard to judge. But when I woke her up, and told her, she looked at me and believed. Maybe there was something about the way I told her, or perhaps it was my voice or my face. Most likely it was because God affirmed this in her heart and mind. She had faith, and knew that I was seeking God, and that God is faithful to come to us in times of need. Being a nurse she was vitally aware of situations when God had intervened to help people in the hospital. She has consistently made it a point to pray with patients and their families. Throughout our lives we have experienced the power of God in answering prayers. In this moment she joined me in prayer, and hugged me as we cried in hope and joy together in trusting the Lord.

During this first month, I went to the doctor's office to have my blood checked on a weekly basis. At first, I underwent chemotherapy and immunotherapy every two weeks. Following these first weeks of intense treatments, the regimen of treatments would be monthly. About six weeks after I had started the chemotherapy I was scheduled for another CT-Scan. This time I would not find out the results until I went to the doctor's office. In my mind I wondered if the tests would show any difference or change. In my heart I trusted that God had done something powerful.

When I went back to the doctor's office to receive the report, Dr. Danish looked over the charts again and again. He then made a phone call to verify the findings. "I can't believe it" he said. "The tumors are gone, and your spleen is almost back to normal. There is no sign of cancer and your blood levels are good." At this point Marilyn and I looked at each other with awareness of that night that I had encountered the Lord, and we said: "Praise God!" "What happened?" asked Dr. Danish. I then told Him that Jesus had come to me one night and had healed me. He then said, "You Christians are different." There was a pause as I almost started to laugh at his comment, but realized that this was Christ's witness to him. "Do you want to continue the treatments?" he asked. For a moment I wondered if he was serious. Beyond the affirmation of being healed by my Savior Jesus Christ, I also knew that I should continue with the complete treatments. I do believe that healing is a coordinated effort of divine intervention and good medical care. So I responded: "Yes, even though I am healed through God's grace, let's finish the treatments." We shook hands as all of us were still in a state of wonder and joy. His staff of nurses rejoiced with us and God was honored and glorified in this intervention of grace and healing. From that point on God used my weekly visits for blood tests and monthly treatment times and doctor visits as a testimony to the other patients and an encouragement to the nursing staff.

That day confirmed the powerful healing and victory I had in Jesus Christ. Marilyn and I rejoiced in the grace and mercy God had shown us. We immediately came home to tell our three sons, and then called family and friends. The word traveled quickly through the church and to many prayer chains in churches that were interceding in prayer around the world. We discovered how broad and yet personal it is to be prayed for in the Body of Christ, locally and worldwide. The prayerful interconnection of believers is closer than we realize. Prayer is a very powerful bond that people share. The good news of my encounter with the living Christ and of God's grace was conveyed. The cancer was no longer detectable. The tumors were gone.

Each time I tell people about this experience of God's personal intervention there is a look of wonder and hope in people's faces. I can not help but be filled with joy every time I recall Christ's glorious brightness. The splendor of His Holiness is magnificent. I will never be the same, and I look forward to seeing Him again. His manifested presence, His glory and grace, love and cleansing presence, have given me assurance and peace, even in the most difficult of moments since then. His very touch imparted healing. Yet beyond the healing there was a deeper joy that permeated my soul, and forever I will turn to Him as my Joy Giver.

Jesus is the Word of God, the very Son of God, the mediator between God and man. Jesus is the Great Physician, the Good Shepherd, the one who reconciles and redeems. When we seek Him we shall find Him. To experience Jesus we may learn from people in Jesus' day who were intentional when it came to seeking Him. They discovered the ministry of grace, truth, and healing that He brought from God the Father. We will not all experience Jesus in exactly the same way. For some it will be the gentle dove of the Holy Spirit that will point the way to the Son of God. For others it will be the brightness of His glory, or the power of His healing touch. Still others will hear His voice, the word of truth, spoken in Scriptures or demonstrated tangibly through the witness of faith in the actions of obedient believers. Those who are battling cancer, and those who are caregivers, may each reflect the glory of our Lord in their faithful hope and obedience. Jesus prayed that the Glory of His Father would be shown through His ultimate sacrifice and passion. He likewise prayed that we would partake in His Glory through our own sacrifice and passion. We all will have tests and trials. Jesus prayed with this awareness. More than anything He prayed for us to be recipients and ambassadors of God's grace and glory.

> *"My prayer is not for them alone. I pray also for those who will believe in me through their message, that all of them may be one, Father, just as you are in me and I am in you. May they also be in us so that the world may believe that you have sent me. I have given them the glory that you gave me, that they may be one as we are one: I in them and you in me. May they be brought to complete unity to let the world know that you sent me and have loved them even as you have loved me. "Father, I want those you have given me to be with me where I am, and to see my glory, the glory you have given me because you loved me before the creation of the world. "Righteous Father, though the world does not know you, I know you, and they know that you have sent me. I have made you known to them, and will continue to make you known in order that the love you have for me may be in them and that I myself may be in them."* (John 17:20-26 NIV)

When God works in our lives we have a choice. We may rejoice in the blessing on simply a personal level, or we may take it further and obediently rejoice in the blessing on a public level. It takes more faith and sweat to take the blessing beyond the personal realm. Jesus did not pray just for the disciples in front of Him, He prayed for the sphere of people beyond their limited vision. He saw people in the world then and people in the future. He saw you and me, in all our sin, brokenness and trouble. In being obedient in prayer and commitment He faced the task in front of Him, to bring about the intervening cure of God for the cancer of human souls and societies. The disciples would come to realize that Jesus was preparing them for their future ministry and witness.

Not thinking only of His own upcoming trial, He prayed for the extension of the gospel. He prayed for people who would come to believe through the shared message. What He would do on the cross, and through the resurrection, would lead them to a saving faith. But salvation is more than the miracles, more than the healing touch, more than the entrance into God's glorious presence. Salvation leads people into a genuine union with God. Salvation also brings about a true unity among people who are quite different from one another in personality and experience. The unifying commonality is a faith relationship with God through Jesus Christ who is Lord and Savior.

That night when the Lord came into my room, resplendent in glory, I experienced transforming fellowship with God. The prayer of Jesus for "those who will believe" was answered. I experienced something that was bigger than I could ever hope to describe, and yet personal enough that I must share what He did in my life. What He did was not simply for me, it was for "those who will believe." The testimony of anyone with faith going through cancer, being healed of cancer, or of anyone dieing with cancer, all have the same focus: "Jesus is with us". Jesus brings us into complete unity with God and one another. With all the brokenness in the world, God uses cancer at times to bring us back into a closer unity with Him and one another. Cancer is a reminder, a messenger, of our mortality and the need for being united into God's trustworthy salvation and love.

5. Trusting in God's Promises Once Again
(Extreme intervention and grace)

There are many things in life that you can neither anticipate nor predict. In the case of my initial battle with cancer, this was an unexpected challenge that God helped us work through. Our faith was made strong as God provided extreme intervention and grace. Little did we know that the lightning bolt of cancer would strike again two years after I was declared to be in full remission.

Thom's story of cancer started on Memorial Day weekend in 2005. At that time Thom was 15 years old and full of vitality. Except for some respiratory issues that we thought were either bronchitis or allergies, we were not aware of the danger that was growing out of control inside his body. His symptoms for several months had involved continual coughing and chest congestion. He also had sinus drainage and headaches. He had seen the doctor twice and the diagnosis was bronchitis and sinus infections. No chest x-ray had been done to look at his lungs. On Friday night of the holiday weekend Thom was entertaining friends at our house when he began to feel very weak and struggled with his breathing. He could not hold food or water, and felt extremely nauseous. These more extreme symptoms seemed to indicate something like pneumonia, and I recalled that Thom had recently been exposed to my father who had pneumonia. After a brief discussion, and having a "gut feeling" that this was something more, I said: "Let's go to the Hospital". We brought him into the emergency room at Genesys Regional Medical Center in Grand Blanc, Michigan.

The initial x-rays showed that his lungs were filled up, and the doctors suggested he be brought to nearby Hurley Hospital's intensive pediatric care unit in Flint. The ambulance came and brought Thom as Marilyn rode along with him. It was about midnight by then, and I followed close behind in our van. As we drove along I wondered how bad his condition was, but the idea of cancer was not in my mind. When we arrived at Hurley Hospital he still felt awful as his breathing was strained. He could not hold food or liquids. By now it was very early in the morning as they settled him into a bed in the pediatric ICU. In a few hours they would do a CT-Scan. I returned home to be with his brothers while Marilyn stayed close by him that night. We were concerned with what appeared to be pneumonia or bronchitis.

On Sunday morning I went to the church and was trying to prepare for worship and preaching, but my mind was not fully focused. I had talked with Marilyn that morning, but I kept my cell phone on just in case. Mark and John came and sat down just before the service started, and then my phone rang just seconds before we were to begin. I went into the back hallway and heard Marilyn in tears explaining that I had to come right away because they found a large mass on Thom's chest. The word "mass" stunned me. How could our son have cancer? It's not something that one can accept or fathom at first. With a heavy heart and a parental sense of urgency I went back into the sanctuary and told the associate minister Rick C. what was going on and that I must leave. I knew that he was capable to take care of the worship and preaching. I then went before the congregation, gave a brief explanation, and then in tears led a prayer for Thom. I excused myself and we went immediately to the hospital. Mark and John were still in shock from the news that I had relayed. I explained further as we got in the car. I told them that there was a mass on Thom's chest and that it was serious and required some immediate decisions and intervention.

In arriving at Hurley, we went up the elevator to the pediatric intensive care unit and saw Thom and Marilyn. A team of doctors came in and indicated that they needed to consult with Marilyn and I. They brought us to a room and

45

showed us the CT-Scan and pointed out where the mass was. "In our opinion it is most probably cancerous", they said, "a fast growing type, and very large, the size of a football (11 x 17 centimeters)." They recommended immediate intervention at a more specialized hospital, the University of Michigan's Mott Children's hospital. In fact, a helicopter was already on the way.

   With everything happening so quickly we were filled with shock, concern and heart-ache. We had to tell Thom what was going on. As we entered the room Thom could read our faces and realized something was seriously wrong. Getting the words out was emotionally heart wrenching, but I told him: "Thom, you have a large tumor in your chest, pressing on your lungs, and they think it is cancerous. They are going to take you by helicopter to U of M hospital." He saw all of us with tears in our eyes and it dawned on him that this was serious. He responded that he believed that he would be alright and said: "Dad, if you were able to be healed of cancer, so can I." We all cried and told Thom how much we loved him, and he told us that he loved us too. We prayed, and soon the helicopter was there and he was whisked up and away. We had to go home and quickly get a few things and drive 53 miles to the Mott Children's Hospital in Ann Arbor at the University of Michigan Medical Center. Even though our world was turned upside down, we had faith in God and gratitude for those helping us.

   In the following writing, Thom reflected upon this experience:

The shocking thing is, it's not all that uncommon. It's happened to a lot more kids than you'd expect, I actually know three other kids that went through the same thing as me. Of course, one of them is dead now.

I was fifteen years old, with less than a month away from my sixteenth birthday, when the doctors diagnosed

46

the large lump in my chest, the one that was pressing up against my heart, lung, and esophagus and preventing about eighty-eight percent of my breathing capacity, as a form of fast-growing, large, diffused B-cell lymphoma. I had cancer, and my doctor thought that I just had bad allergies.

A lot of people think of cancer as a death sentence; they think that coupled along with the words "you have cancer" are the words "you have three months to live", or however many months the doctors feel like throwing at you. So what runs through your head when someone is essentially giving you your time of death? What ran through my head was, "I think I should call someone and tell them, that way they know where I am and why I'm not at school." Wow, I'm a loser.

I looked around me as I was thinking about who to call. My family was breaking down in tears. My mother wept and held me, my father comforted the both of us; my older brother sat down and tried to fight it initially, and my younger brother stood off to the side of my bed and just watched me with tears streaming down his face. I don't remember if I cried, at the time I didn't realize I should have been crying.
The only thing that popped into my head was "hand me a phone", and they did. I called my friend Josh and left a message on their answering machine, something to the effect of, "Hey, it's Thom...I'm at the hospital now and they say I have cancer, so...tell everyone." Maybe I threw in something about school, I can't remember now.
The doctors told my parents some options, all I remember is that their options were basically "You have to go to U of M Hospital now." Apparently, that now was just urgent enough for me to be air-lifted. This was the first time I have ever ridden in a helicopter, and it was an amazing experience. I'll never forget the look on

the faces of my mother and older brother as I felt myself being lifted into the air by the two blades whirring loudly above my head: they looked so uncertain, so confused and worried. My mom almost looked like she was watching my body ascend into heaven.

Oh, I forgot to mention: at this point, if I were to lie down I was incapable of breathing.

When we arrived in Ann Arbor at the University hospital, the team of flight nurses in their blue jumpsuits wheeled my stretcher up to the ICU of Mott Children's hospital. Waiting for me in my room were my Uncle Paul, Aunt Audrey, and my cousins David and Kelly. They live in Ypsilanti so they were able to keep me company until my parents arrived about thirty minutes later. During the thirty minutes before my parents arrived, a mass of about twenty or thirty doctors had coagulated at my hospital room door. They were all discussing, in a rather doctor-ish manner, what they were to do with me. I didn't hear very much of what they were talking about, I don't think I would have wanted to anyways.

Before I continue, it's vital that you know this: if the doctors administered any pain medication to me at this point, because of the fluid that had built up in my lungs and the precarious location of the mass within my ribcage, I could die.

As soon as my parents arrived, a doctor who had emerged from the pack as the leader handed them a few papers and ushered them with some hushed words. I watched as they signed the papers and my extended family was rushed outside. My family came in briefly and offered me a few words of encouragement. Frankly, I don't remember any of it because of what happened next. The lead doctor came into the room accompanied by another doctor or two and a handful of nurses. My mother asked if she could stay; she's a nurse trained in intensive care.

Now, someone probably explained to me what was about to happen, but all I could remember was my mother telling me to keep breathing as the plastic tube was stabbed into my side, between my ribs, and into my lung. I screamed. Everything went black.
I heard voices. I peeled my eyes open and saw a bunch of doctors standing around me in a very sterile looking room. I turned to the one closest to me and mumbled "If I die it's your fault" as nonchalantly as if I was saying "I'd like a double-cheese burger and a chocolate shake."
"You're not going to die," the doctor told me, and I replied "Okay" and everything went black again.
I felt that I was in a bed again, but I could tell I wasn't wearing pants anymore. I asked why I was naked, but all I heard was laughter then silence again.

I heard voices again, this time one male and one female voice. The male voice was instructing the female voice on how to put something somewhere. Then I felt a sharp pain and loudly and urgently inquired what they were doing to me.
Finally my eyes opened and everything was clear. My family was around me, and they remained around me for the rest of my treatment and ever since. I love them all dearly and will miss them every day that I'm gone making something out of the second chance that I've been given.

God worked in Thom's life. We were blessed with a deeper love for one another and a deeper faith in God. We were also blessed with a stronger sense of being lifted up by a supportive community of people. While Thom's experience involved traumatic intervention, pain and discomfort, he was not alone or unsupported.

The importance of supportive care during a life-threatening time must be intentionally shown through a vigilant and caring presence. As a pastor I have noted that those patients who had the support of family and community did much better than those who lacked support and caring presence. God indeed calls people to be partners, participants, and prayerful coaches in His work of intervention and healing. The blessings that come through such experiences help us to be in touch with our calling and purpose to be God's hands, hearts, voices, and vessels of compassion in action.

Thom went through a difficult battle while he was at the hospital on and off for eight months. After the first week of watching his lungs continually drain through bilateral chest tubes (which included special measurable containers that were placed on both sides of his bed), we wondered if this draining would ever stop. It turned out that his lymphatic duct was being blocked by the still growing tumor, causing certain things he ate (primarily fats) to be redirected into his lungs. In addition to this, he still had the pericardial drain extracting fluids that had accumulated at the lining his heart.

The doctor's were nervous because the work of pathology, to determine what type of cancer he had, was going slow because they could not obtain a normal biopsy. With the tumor pressing on his airway, surgery was out of the question (no intubation was safe). They had to rely upon samples obtained through the fluid that drained from his lungs, and from a small biopsy obtained externally. All this made the diagnosis difficult and the staff physicians anxious because the tumor was still growing.

The initial reports from the doctors were devastating. One resident came in and told us that they believed Thom had either a Sarcoma or a T-Cell

50

Lymphoma. He explained that either of these held little hope for the success of treatments. The one thing that presented some potential for slowing it down was radiation. Since the tumor was close to his heart this would be risky. The doctor who gave us the bad news left Marilyn and I alone in the room as tears welled up and our hopes were dashed. I don't think I have ever felt so low and so broken-hearted. We had each other to bear this burden, but at this point we experienced the pain that so many parents go through in grieving with the death or impending death of their own child. There is no question that a parent's loss of a child is the hardest grief to experience. As much as the visit of some friends that day was appreciated, they could not fully understand what we were feeling. The comment that "this is not about you, but all about God's working" was true, but not so sensitive. In fact, God does enter in to help us with our personal needs, especially when we are broken and in need of His personal grace and comfort. In a very real way, it is "about us" and His redemptive care in times of crisis and pain. We were in great need and God comforted us, mostly through His direct loving presence and promises. The eternal promise of salvation held us together, that God prepares a place for us through Jesus Christ the risen Lord. We were sure of Thom's salvation because he was a believer, and though we were grieving, we were assured of the power of our resurrected Lord who prepares a place for those who believe and know Him as Savior. Nonetheless, our pain was real and we had to rely upon the comfort of the Holy Spirit with groans and tears that words could not express.

The next day we spoke with the other doctors involved with the case and they gave us more hope. Indeed, they suggested that radiation treatment should be started soon. The time was scheduled and tests were done to determine exactly where and how the radiation should proceed. The day came for the radiation treatment; it was on a weekday afternoon. We had called all family and friends, and our church, to be vigilant in prayer.

Holding hands, we prayed with Thom, and then they brought him down through the maze of hallways to the radiation treatment room. Once Thom was lying on the x-ray table, they marked his chest with an ink pen, drawing a cross at the center of his chest which was to be the exact site of radiation. We were invited to wait with the pathologist in his office nearby. We continued in prayer. Just a few minutes before he was scheduled to begin radiation, the phone in the pathologist's office rang; he picked it up and then darted out of the room. He ran to the radiation room yelling "Stop! Stop!" as he banged on the door. When the door opened he looked relieved that he had gotten there in time, and that they were just seconds away from starting the radiation treatment. They stopped the procedure and we were brought into a conference room. The doctors then informed us that the pathology results had just come in with a more accurate diagnosis. Thom did not have one of those other types of deadly cancers, he had a treatable "Large Diffused B-Cell Non-Hodgkin's Lymphoma." The doctors explained that this kind of cancer did not need to be treated with radiation, but could be treated through chemotherapy and immunotherapy. We realized in this moment of grace that our prayers had been answered and that there was hope. Thom was taken from the table and brought back to his room. The doctor's could start making plans for how to treat him using the protocol that had been effective for his type of cancer. We realized that he was just seconds away from being radiated, and God intervened. The site of the radiation had involved a risk, and may have resulted in damage to his heart. The timing and intervention of this news from pathology was a miracle, a timely act of mercy and grace. The light of hope was dawning once again.

With hope for Thom's prognosis came renewed peace and joy. Our hearts that were so burdened were now uplifted. Though we knew that it was not over yet, and many challenges were still ahead of Thom and us, we trusted in God's presence, power and providential working. Certainly at our lowest points of life God is not unaffected by our cry for mercy and grace. Whether the intervention of God involves a means for healing that extends life physically, or a transforming end that receives life back unto our eternal home of care, we must trust and have faith in God's sovereignty and power. At that moment of diagnosis and intervention we were fully aware of God's protective and providential hand being at work.

Why God intervenes with a means for healing for some and why others do not receive a means for healing is difficult to understand. For sure, our hearts break when the healing or a cure we are looking for is absent. Yet in some way, this sense of the unknown leads us to desire, and rest more fully upon, God's ultimate cure and healing that is promised in the resurrection and eternal life offered through Jesus Christ. For us, in a deeper way, we were brought face to face with death so that we would affirm life eternal. The powerful truth we once again grasped was the ultimate hope we have come to know and trust personally through our Savior, Jesus Christ. We were prepared for the death of Thom, but the author of life chose to extend his life. Why? The reasons are still unfolding, but we have discovered that God reveals His glory in and through the challenges of our lives. Whether we live or die when faced with cancer, the choice of faith allows us to know and glorify God regardless of our prognosis, or length of life, after the diagnosis and treatment. At the core of our being we are called into God's work of grace. Sometimes God even uses cancer to bring us near to His heart.

Ultimately, the challenges of life call for faith in God. Cancer is but one of many reminders that we are mere mortals in need of God's saving grace. It's not that cancer is the sin, but that cancer is the result of a broken and sinful world where the creation itself has been corrupted. Our bodies, as well as the created order of this earth, have been polluted by the consequence of humanity's sinful choices that started in the Garden of Eden. While many people will avoid this factor when considering cancer, it remains evident that God calls us to be participants in His redemptive work for creation. This means that God will actually seek to bless us when cancer is detected. God calls for us to be partners in His work of redemption and healing. Not all cancer can be eliminated, but many cancers can be treated, contained, and conquered. Much like the sins of greed, hatred, jealousy, boastfulness, envy, slander, gossip, or dishonesty, cancer can be dealt with through identification, acknowledgement, and intervention. God is at work to help those who battle cancer, for in this battle we are engaged in a very personal struggle with the redemption of our bodies.

This matter of the redemption of our bodies is comparable to the work of God to redeem mankind. Consider what the Apostle Paul wrote to the Roman believers who struggled with a corrupt and cancerous society that tortured and martyred them:

Yet what we suffer now is nothing compared to the glory he will give us later. For all creation is waiting eagerly for that future day when God will reveal who his children really are. Against its will, everything on earth was subjected to God's curse. All creation anticipates the day when it will join God's children in glorious freedom from death and decay. For we know that all creation has been groaning as in the pains of childbirth right up to the present time. (Romans 8:18-22)

Paul could not tell them that redemption was an immediate cure, but that it was a process in progress through Jesus Christ the Savior. In this process we go through suffering, but ultimately faith in God leads us to experience the glory of God through His restoration and redemption of humanity as His children. For now we realize that the earth is subject to a curse that resulted because of evil corrupting humanity. Why evil even exists is another related issue, one that defies our limited understanding. Yet in spite of the corruption that resulted in man's disobedience of God, there is hope in God's initiative of salvation. God loves us and calls humanity to repentance and redemption. God is able to heal. Likewise, the Lord calls humanity to participate in His healing. God is compassionate and loving, and the Lord calls humanity to be compassionate and loving. God is revealing a plan through Jesus Christ that will result in the redemption of this earth and those who are His people, who are remade in His image through faith. What the risen Lord offers as a gift is "freedom from death and decay." The groaning we experience now will give way to "the glory He will give us" in time as we trust and believe. This glory is not contingent upon a cure, but is granted in the blessing of God's constant care and abiding love. This matter of trusting in God's promises becomes essential when dealing with chemotherapy, or any type of medical treatment that entails suffering, discomfort, and difficult recovery. The hope of redemption for our souls and our bodies is the essence of God's work of grace.

In the preceding chapters we focused upon the experience and development of "faith" as the starting point for discovering the blessings that may come through having cancer. The "soul fruit" of faith is given by God's Spirit and will lead to all of the other "fruits of the Spirit" that God can develop in us as we rely upon His strength and grace. This is true in the battle with cancer, as well as true with any other experience of adversity or challenge. Therefore, in the following chapters I will write more specifically about how God is involved in developing "soul fruit". To reinforce the point, please note that I will draw upon the "fruit of the Spirit" identified by the Apostle Paul in two places. First, Paul wrote to the church in Corinth, where in chapter 13 he concluded with the revelation that

"*Faith, Hope, and Love*" abide in spirit-filled persons. In conclusion he affirmed that the greatest of these three is "Love". Second, Paul wrote to the Galatians, Chapter 5, verse 22-23, saying "*But when the Holy Spirit controls our lives, he will produce this kind of fruit in us: love, joy, peace, patience, kindness, goodness, faithfulness, gentleness, and self-control.*" In a saving relationship with God we have a foundation through "faith" for "soul fruit". From faith we may grow into the next fruit of the Spirit; moving forward we will explore "hope".

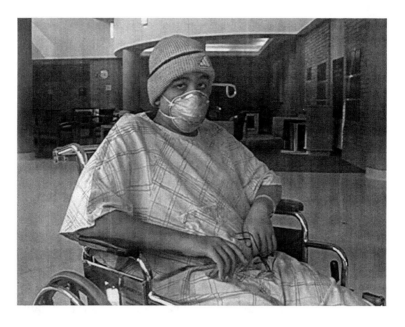

Thom at Mott Children's Hospital, wearing a knit cap given by his grandfather Gene Arnold.

6. Believing Beyond What is Seen
(Bearing the blessing of hope)

Where does hope come from? What leads us to deeply need hope for the future? Hope involves the elements of being, belonging, and becoming. We are not mere creatures living for the moment who have no regard to dreams, visions, or goals. We are made with the need to connect past, present and future. We are designed by our creator with a desire to live "beyond" ourselves and toward possibilities and growth. Our design is connected with the communities that we fellowship within, as our hope is rooted in the extension of this fellowship within time and throughout time. Our creator God made us in His image with hope in mind.

When God first instructed Adam and Eve, He gave them a message of hope and purpose. God said: "bear fruit and multiply", go and "subdue" the earth (Genesis 1:28). We are called by our Creator to grow and bear fruit in life with hope and vision. We are invited by our Creator/Father to participate in creation with hope and vitality. Though as a human race we had fallen to sin and corruption, God's mandate and blessing of hope remained. The fulfillment of this hope may now be found in a redemptive partnership that we must grow into through the journey of salvation. The blessing of believing beyond the cancer involves a hope in God. This hope is actualized in God's revelation of Himself through His Son, the Savior, Jesus Christ.

Greater than any test is the testimony of God's presence and love. Beyond the CT Scans, PET Scans, Gallium Scans, ultrasounds, blood tests, x-rays, and pathology work done through microscopes there is a Great Physician, Jesus Christ. Beyond what we see and know, God is there. Believing in the blessing of good medical help is part of the hope. Yet beyond the working of man there is the unseen presence and power of God, His Holy

Spirit, and His very own Son Jesus Christ.   You may choose to believe, or not to believe in this, but still the question tugs at you, "Where do you place your hope?" Every person needs hope for it is essential to our humanity. Yet somehow we can't ignore the connection that our need for hope provides evidence to our spiritual nature and origin. We all have a yearning for something more; indeed we are created to be united with the one who created us.

I remember talking to one very helpful doctor at University of Michigan's Mott Children's Hospital, Dr. Jeff Fleming. He was a key person during the initial emergency intervention at the Pediatric Intensive Care Unit. He was the one who helped coordinate the team that first stabilized our son. He was the one who steadied Thom as he inserted a tube into Thom's left chest to drain the fluids from his lungs. He was the one who exuded hope and confidence, who took time to encourage us from his experience in helping other children with similar situations. He was the one who explained all that was going on, and stayed close by for our first week in the hospital. One night while Thom was sleeping, Dr. Jeff sat down next to me during a quiet time in the intensive care unit and we talked for nearly two hours about life, hope, and God.   I asked him: "Where do you place your hope?"   He answered: "I believe in the work of people and of good medicine. I do believe there is a higher power at work, but God works for healing through people who apply their knowledge." Dr. Jeff acknowledged that hope involves both knowledge and a higher power, and that this higher power leads us to expand and apply our knowledge.   Whether he was aware of it or not, he was operating out of an unseen hope. While I agree that hope exists in using our available knowledge and medical practices that have shown to be effective, I also believe that hope exists apart from the known or the previously tried treatments.   If not, we would not venture to seek new treatments or procedures.   If hope was simply using our available knowledge, then it would not be hope at all.

"Who hopes for what he already has?" (Romans 8:24)   Dr. Jeff left the door open to "the higher power".   Ultimately, hope is rooted in the author of life and healing.   Since our knowledge is imperfect it stands to reason that our hope is being perfected.   How so?   Since knowledge increases through research, experience and treatment development, then too our hope for providing healing through medical means increases over time.   However, this process of improving cancer diagnosis and treatment is not without a foundation, and that foundation is the presence of hope itself.   This hope is rooted in someone/something greater than ourselves, with knowledge and power that are beyond our current knowledge or practices.   Because of this we believe that there are breakthroughs, miracles, and interventions.   Though we may not always find healing or a cure, we may still maintain hope beyond what we see. *"Hope that is seen is no hope at all."* (Romans 8:24)

Our experience with cancer revealed that hope involves a focus ultimately upon God.   Now God works through people within the medical, religious, and human service community, but God also works above and beyond doctors and researchers.   Although my fourth stage cancer was overwhelming, still my hope connected me to God, who gave me great peace and joy.   Thom's cancer was severe and life-threatening, and still our hope sustained us through the grief and trials we would face.   We hoped for the healing that we did not yet have, but which God would provide.   If healing did not involve the physical restoration of health, our hope was still secure in the hope of the resurrection and of eternal life.   Still, we believed that we would see the hand of God work to reveal His grace and glory.   We believed that God was at work specifically and personally, and we saw the hand of God work through medical and hospital personnel.

God is bigger than cancer. By faith we would face our health concerns with hope in the one who creates and redeems. Inevitably, there will be some pain, brokenness, struggle, doubt, fear, or grief that we may experience. However, our calling and purpose is to face these difficult realities with courage and hope. Once again, encouragement for the battle originates from the One who made heaven and earth, the One who is life-giving and life-sustaining.

For the most part, the other parents of the children of cancer that we met at University of Michigan maintained hope while remaining courageous. Still, underneath the surface, parents would at times honestly share their struggles, frustrations, despair, and doubts. This process of honest admission was itself an expression of hope and of needing the support of community. What concerned me more was when people didn't talk, but held it in and stayed to themselves. It seems that hope exists where people stay connected and communicative. Hope diminishes where people become isolated and disconnected. Hope in God is comparable in that as people stay in communion with God and the community of believers, their faith, hope, and love will remain. But if people put up barriers to God and others it will negatively affect them more than they realize, and hope shall diminish.

The experience of having a child go through a battle with cancer can either make or break your sense of hope. For some, the experience deepens and positively develops their character, for others it is deeply painful or paralyzing. At times cancer caregivers or patients can become fixated on blaming, resentment, envy, anger, despair, or fear. The dark side of going through a battle with cancer must be acknowledged if there is to be hope. The key is not to ignore these monsters, but to slay them through faith, hope, and love. Once again, hope opens the way to our connection with God and to the community of care and treatment that God provides. The healthiest thing we can do when faced with our pain is not to curl up and retreat from all others, but it is to seek help and support. This is why support groups and conversations with others are so essential. Our character is therefore developed best in the context of community, and that itself is a gift from our creator who said: "*Let us make mankind in our image*" (Genesis 1:26 NIV). Note that God created all life and humanity itself from His divine community. Our likeness to God is not only spiritual, it is also relational. Note that when Jesus faced the cruelty of sinful humanity and chose to bear our sins on the cross, He called out for help and understanding from His Heavenly Father. He likewise identified with our brokenness and alienation when He quoted Psalm 22, "*My God, My God, why have You forsaken me?*" He ministered God's grace in the spirit of reconciliation and healing when He said: "*Father, forgive them, for they know not what they do*" Luke 23:34 NIV). Jesus cared about His mother as He called out to His closest friend "John" and told him to take care of Mary as if she was his own mother. Throughout His crucifixion Jesus revealed empathy. Even greater than His immediate care for His mother Mary, His sacrificial atonement embodied and promoted healing and hope for all of lost humanity. Through His forgiving words and work, Jesus envisioned that we were future participants of God's covenant community through His Father's grace.

One of Thom's revelations through his experience was that God shows Himself through people. He came to the conclusion that one of the greatest proofs of God's existence is the incredible diversity and complexity of humanity. In the beauty, complexity, and even in man's free will, something of God's image is revealed. We are not mere robots, we are "*fearfully and wonderfully made*" as the Psalmist notes (Psalm 139:14). For Thom, he has experienced the highs and lows of battling cancer. He has seen the best and worst of life. He sees life with the experience of facing death. Through all of this his hope has not diminished, but has grown. The soul fruit of Hope is often born from adversity as one senses the presence and activity of a "Higher Power". Some people work hard to maintain a stance that the source of hope is nameless for the sake of not making a commitment of faith. Still others work hard to keep the identity of hope's source anonymous for the sake of not offending people of different religions. Personally, I can't help but celebrate the specific revelation of God our Father in Jesus Christ His Son and the Holy Spirit. This Triune revelation of God, this Divine community, is actively pursuing humanity with a ministry and message of hope.

For those facing cancer their experience of hope will vary according to what is at the center of their lives. Without faith in Jesus Christ you may have hope that is good, but this hope may not be eternally connected. We may hope to regain the things we have had, or renew and improve the relationships and lives we cherish. This is good, but it still does not connect us directly to the author of life and heaven. We may hope for good things, but our hope may only be temporal at that point. Winning the fight with cancer can only bring temporary victory. The need for a greater hope is found beyond the temporal blessings of this life, and is experienced through the fruit of God's Spirit as one may walk in faith. God loves us and wants to fellowship with us. In the hope of salvation given by Jesus there is a plan and purpose that extends beyond any battle with cancer. Our hope is in God's unseen presence and trustworthy working of grace.

One of our favorite Scripture verses on hope is in Jeremiah 29:11-14. *For I know the plans I have for you," says the LORD. "They are plans for good and not for disaster, to give you a future and a hope. [12] In those days when you pray, I will listen. [13] If you look for me in earnest, you will find me when you seek me. [14]I will be found by you," says the LORD. (New Living Translation)*

To know that God has plans for those who battle cancer may be difficult to accept or fathom, especially when all that seems to be evident is the disease or the *"valley of the shadow of death"* (Psalm 23). Nevertheless, the truth we may hold on to is the *"For I know"* of God. The *"plans"* may be hidden from us, but they are not hidden from God. They are plans for *"good and not for disaster"*(Jeremiah 29:11). How can you be sure that God will give a future and a hope? The answer comes in verses 12 and 13: *"when you pray, I will listen...you will find me when you seek me."* Hope is rooted in the God who gives us the potential of faith. Prayer is therefore critically essential if we are to receive the gift of a bright future and hope on earth and most of all in God's Heavenly Kingdom. This bright future many times involves healing and the future wellness of body, mind and soul. However, this future for all of us will inevitably mean having a hope that takes us beyond this life itself. Ultimately the greatest hope, the greatest healing, the greatest victory is in the power of Jesus Christ's atoning death and resurrection. From God's Son we may receive the fully realized hope of God's transformation for eternal life.

To find God is hope indeed. This hope transcends our pain, our losses, our grief, our sorrow, our disappointments, our frustrations, our fears, our trials. In releasing our struggles and battle with cancer to God, and through the support of people God had placed around us, we discovered that hope is an unfolding gift. Hope in God brings the healing and empowering perspective of faith. As a result, the darkness of doubt and despair is progressively dispelled and defeated, put into the realm of being temporary. The Apostle Paul referred to this when he wrote to the Corinthians:

So we fix our eyes not on what is seen, but on what is unseen.
For what is seen is temporary, but what is unseen is eternal.
II Corinthians 4:18 (NIV)

7. Discovering a Love that Endures
(Bearing the blessing of enduring love)

Many times I would walk into the chemo unit of Mott Children's hospital early in the morning and find Marilyn and Thom sleeping, trying to catch some much needed rest. Marilyn and I would take turns staying with Thom overnight, but to her credit, she was the most vigilant. Her enduring love and medical awareness were appreciated by Thom and I, who understood that she would watch his treatments and condition carefully. Thom grew to appreciate the blessing of being cared for. We grew to understand that there is great joy in not only giving, but in receiving the love and care of others. We came to appreciate how God had placed many capable people to assist and care for Thom. All of this reinforced the enduring love of God, and the blessing reflected through the enduring love of people. Certainly when the environment of a cancer patient is both supportive and encouraging, the outcome is often more positive. Let's consider how love is to be expressed, understood, and received.

The Apostle Paul wrote to the church in Corinth with a prescription for helping them overcome various "cancerous sins" that threatened their health as a community of faith. He told them that they needed faith, hope, and love to battle the cancerous development of pride, envy, boastfulness, rudeness, irritability, resentment and doubt. In fact, the greatest of these "spiritual" therapies is "love". Paul went on to affirm that: *"Love never gives up, never loses faith, is always hopeful, and endures through every circumstance."* (I Corinthians 13:7 NLT) In fact, while faith and hope are essential for healing, love is the greatest of the three. Love brings us into communion with God, and love defines the very essence of God. Since we are made in the image of God, the potential for growing in God's love is the very substance of hope realized through faith. *"For God so loved the world that He gave his only Son, so that everyone who believes in Him will not perish but have eternal life. [17]God did not send his Son into the world to condemn it, but to save it."* (John 3:16-17 NLT)

We discovered afresh the enduring love of God throughout the days when both Thom and I battled cancer. God worked through people and also worked in our hearts. In the midst of being challenged we drew upon the love of our Lord as the source of strength. God's love endures as the sure foundation of life. There is nothing that can separate us from God's love when we abide in our Savior Jesus Christ. Yes, cancer would test us. Yet God's presence and power, His very mercy and provision, would sustain us. While cancer is but a temporary reminder of our mortality, cancer is ultimately under the control of God. God allows this disease to exist and in turn it serves to test us, and through faith cancer may bring us closer to our redeemer God. In that way cancer may even serve to bear blessings when we are drawn to discover, and respond to, God's love. Before detection, after diagnosis, and through treatments one may rely upon the Lord.

The most important end result of prayer is not necessarily a cure, although we may desire this with hope. The end result we are offered as we face trials, disease, or sin is a movement toward full deliverance that comes from the saving grace of God. The revelation of God's saving love was made personal in the very coming and ministry of Jesus the Christ. The grace of God was given through Him so that we may have life through the gift of God's redeeming love. What Jesus accomplished on the cross was prescriptive to heal our sin-sick, cancerous, souls, not just our sick bodies. Jesus is the Great Physician we need in order to be restored spiritually, but also to bear fruit within our souls spiritually. His authority and ministry as the Son of God is trustworthy. We may turn to Jesus at any time to find God's eternal and enduring love. Jesus spoke words of invitation in the book of Revelation that tell us that He is still initiating a relationship with all of mankind:

Here I am! I stand at the door, and knock. If anyone hears my voice and opens the door, I will come in and eat with him, and he with me. To him who overcomes, I will give the right to sit with me on my throne, just as I overcame and sat down with my Father on His throne. (Revelation 3:20-21 NIV)

Through faith in Christ we shall overcome the trials of cancer, and the result will be that we shall receive honor in Heaven. For now we are promised something wonderful, sweet communion with God through knowing Jesus Christ. In this relationship of love with our Lord, our souls will be revitalized even if our bodies are wasting away. There is great fruit for the soul that no cancer can steal or spoil, fruit that will last even beyond this life. Facing cancer has deeply challenged us to be completely open to the presence and power of Jesus. In seeking the face of Jesus we have come into direct contact with God and His love. Can there be a greater blessing than this? For it was from this very battle with cancer that we entered into a greater experience of God's loving deliverance, God's eternal love.

When we were first given the diagnosis of cancer, both for me and for Thom, the first order of concern was to show love and support for one another. This is a reflection of the fact that love is the most primary and greatest of spiritual gifts. When we love one another unconditionally, even sacrificially, it mirrors the reality that we are made in the image of God. God prioritizes His love for us, as do we for one another, as we face times of crisis. God is an ever-present, never failing, trustworthy, strength, the One who gives hope and healing.

In the midst of being loved by God, we are still confronted by one who is lower than God, whose rebellion is experienced in his adversarial relationship with God and those of God's Kingdom. Evil, authored by the corrupter Satan, is ultimately no match for God and those of whom God's love is indwelling. While cancer is a chaotic corruption of our body's cells, it cannot destroy the soul or spirit of a person. A doctor can regulate the treatments that will fight these chaotic and corrupted cells, but a doctor cannot fight moral or spiritual chaos through medical means. I observed some patients in the chemo clinic who were winning their temporary battle with cancer, but were losing their eternally essential battle with sin. The demeanor, words, or lifestyle of people would continue to evidence anger, hostility, rebellion, pride, or denial of their need for God. Once again, here is where affirming and discovering the love of God in Jesus Christ is essential. Ultimate victory from spiritual cancer, sin, is given to those who believe in the Lord Jesus Christ. A battle with physical cancer may indeed bring us to a breaking point, and ultimately into a relationship of greater reliance upon the love of God and the supportive love of others.

One of God's blessings we have experienced through dealing with cancer has been the increased intentionality of expressing our love for one another. Our family communication is regularly seasoned with three vital words: "I love you." We have realized that life is fragile and that it is essential to express love directly and frequently. Furthermore, we have realized that conversations need to be more in-depth and honest, whereby we can help one another. The importance of the quality of our care and communication has increased as we have grown in loving one another. This is not to say we have perfected our communication, we still have room for great improvement. The quality of life we share as a family has implications for how we apply ourselves to love others within the broader community. We continue to appreciate the bigger family God has given us for support. Cancer has catapulted us into a network of care. Within this broader community we have been blessed with companionship, fellowship of suffering, kindness, understanding, inspiration, and supportive friendship.

The Relay for Life events are a good example of how cancer survivors and their care givers and supporters make up a loving family. People in some towns set up their campers and stay overnight. They make up a supportive, even mission minded, network. Friends and family, people of all ages, come together to raise money and awareness. But more importantly, they build community by cheering on the fighters of cancer, rejoicing with the victors, while also bearing the shared pain of those who have lost loved ones. These events are not morbid parades; they are encouraging harbors of hope for the future. The survivor walks are very emotional for those of us who are living testimonies of the success of cancer research and treatment. I remember the first time I walked in a Relay for Life. I had just survived my 6 months of therapy and was declared cancer free. The organizers of the event asked me to speak at the event before the walk. I looked out to the faces of people I knew, most of whom had prayed for me and my family. In speaking to this community of support, I expressed my deep gratitude. Then, in walking the circuit beside the other survivors, I was deeply moved by the cheering, clapping, crowd of people who lined our path. My mind moved with a vision toward a future time, that I believe people of saving faith will experience, when God's redeemed shall be welcomed home to Heaven with a parade of victory. Coming back to earth, as I stumbled a bit on the gravel road, I heard people call out my name, and the name of others next to me. I was reminded that we do not fight cancer in vain, or alone. Even if my cancer returned some day, and for some reason I could not walk with my fellow survivors in person, I knew that I would always walk with them in spirit. Even better, we may look forward to the ultimate healing of the resurrection, and the homecoming of the redeemed in Heaven.

When my son Thom and I were joined together in his first survivor walk, I noticed that he felt awkward at first, and then I noticed that he was deeply moved by the realization that both of us were blessed to be supported by a loving community. People called out his name; friends had gathered in a tent in his honor and had a party of celebration and support. I looked at my son walking next to me and felt great admiration for his courage. My wife and I were among the few who understood what a walking miracle he was. Through the steps we walked together I counted it all a blessing to share a bond of suffering and healing with my son. Deeper still was the bond of faith, hope, and love. This bond would not have been as strong had we not both endured similar hardships. We could count it all joy in that we were more than survivors; we were over comers. God had showed us the greater value of life in His big family. The journey around the track symbolized new hope, a new beginning, a trust and faith in how God had not only walked alongside us, but had gone before us to prepare the way. Thom's friends, many who came to the hospital in his darkest hours, had raised money for cancer research in his honor. They stood up as Thom approached their group. They ran to the edge of the road and then loudly cheered, clapped, whistled, and yelled out in loving abandon: "We love you Thom."

Who is there for you? Who is calling out your name? Who is cheering for you when the times are difficult, or you celebrate victory? Who is bearing with your suffering, and helping to bear your load of pain or trouble? Think about it. Pray about it. God answers in love and touches us through those He sends.

69

8. Nurturing a Joy that Strengthens
(*Bearing the blessing of joy*)

"Supportive Sisters"

Happiness and Joy were sisters

Happiness left home in pursuit of something that was lacking
Joy stayed home, graduated, and started her life with education
and a purpose

Happiness had extreme ups and downs
Joy was steady and faithful

Happiness changed according to what was happening at the
moment
Joy found strength to manage and learn through every situation

Happiness found it hard to live up to her name
Joy looked to God to help her make a good name

Happiness and Joy both developed cancer

Happiness could not accept what was happening to her
Joy had peace to accept what God had allowed for her

Happiness realized that she needed help
Joy knew where to find help

Happiness found Joy, together they survived cancer
Happiness was blessed with Joy, Joy was blessed with Happiness

Poem by Scott Arnold, 8-2008

    The poem above affirms that the fruit of the Spirit
"Joy" is the result of one's faith in God and is the resulting
development of spiritual character. Joy may be a simple

and beautiful gift that is apparent in children. But the influence of evil in the world, and the pain of sin and brokenness, eventually attempts to steal, choke, or cloud this gift. To protect the gift of joy it takes faith, a positive attitude, discipline, and the support of others. To reacquire the gift of joy it takes renewal or reception of joy based upon faith. The Apostle Paul concluded his letter to the Romans by praying that they would have "Joy". *May the God of hope fill you with all joy and peace as you trust in him, so that you may overflow with hope by the power of the Holy Spirit.* Romans 15:13 (NIV)

Joy comes from trusting God to fill our hearts and lives with goodness and grace. Joy is closely related to happiness, and is the source of true and lasting happiness. But the difference is critical in that happiness is fleeting, while joy is sustaining and everlasting. Joy runs deeper because it is a spiritual gift that is connected to a source greater than our selves. Joy springs forth from our Creator as help for our souls, and is the silent strength that sustains us when troubles arise, fears are confronted, and suffering is experienced.

Joy is also drawn upon as a matter of choice, believing that life's blessing is greater than life's pain and disappointment. Joy involves a response to bless and not curse. To rejoice is contingent upon having a source of joy from which to share one's joy with others. Since joy is an expression of wonder, gratitude, faith, and hope, the source of such goodness and joy is not just within us. Joy that is lasting is a gift from the Lord our God. Therefore, even with the diagnosis of cancer we may choose the path of faith that says: *"Rejoice in the Lord always, and again I say, rejoice!* (Philippians 4:4 NIV). The ability to have joy in the midst of trials and illness is therefore contingent upon our faith outlook. Jesus comforted His disciples as He talked honestly about His upcoming death and resurrection, as He promised them joy: *"You will grieve, but your grief will turn to joy."* John 16:20 (NIV).

71

Jesus did not deny that we will grieve, but revealed that sin and grief will be overcome by joy.

As a pastor I have counseled and visited many people in times of crisis. I have wept with those who have faced pain and loss. I have rejoiced with those who have discovered salvation and love. I have been gratefully received as well as distained and rejected, even by those who proclaim the same faith and Savior. I have seen God moving in powerful ways to transform lives and give hope in Christ, but I have also seen people hate and destroy one another as a result of a lack of joy and peace. I can relate with the Apostle Paul as he wrote from Rome's prison to the Philippians, saying:

> *⁴ Rejoice in the Lord always. I will say it again: Rejoice! ⁵ Let your gentleness be evident to all. The Lord is near. ⁶ Do not be anxious about anything, but in everything, by prayer and petition, with thanksgiving, present your requests to God. ⁷ And the peace of God, which transcends all understanding, will guard your hearts and your minds in Christ Jesus.*
> Philippians 4:4-7 (NIV)

Again and again I have learned that my joy is rooted not in people, but in the Lord. My peace in Christ is not a construction of well-wishing, but is a transcendent awareness and strength born out of faith where joy is met and confronted by suffering. Through my own battle with cancer, and through my son's battle with cancer, it was the joy of the Lord that has been our strength. You may say, "Well it's easy to have joy when you have been healed, when you have been the recipient of miracles. But where was God when my loved one died with cancer? Where is God now as I deal with incurable cancer?" To these questions and more I have also walked in darkness. No one can dismiss the painful reality of death. Even Jesus wept as He prayed for the salvation of Jerusalem and all nations for which He gave His life for. To these concerns of facing suffering and pain I must share more personally of how my brother Bruce maintained joy while facing his death with cancer.

Bruce was a successful optometrist in our home town of Midland, Michigan. He was also joyfully married to his wife Christina, and enjoyed his two daughters Elizabeth and Valerie. He was my oldest brother, and someone that I looked up to for intelligence and wisdom. In his early 30's Bruce was diagnosed with Kidney cancer. They had found a tumor near one of his kidneys that was already large and required risky surgery at Mayo Clinic. The surgery was deemed a success, and he was declared cancer-free. The future looked hopeful and optimistic regarding his long term prognosis. He came to a deeper faith in God and a personal relationship with Jesus Christ as a result of his battle with cancer. Several years later, when the cancer returned, he maintained the joy he had discovered in trusting Jesus Christ before. All throughout his last 5-6 years of battling cancer, this time through difficult immunotherapy and chemotherapy, he remained positive and joyful toward life. Toward the end of his fight, at age 39, he shared with me that he was ready to go to heaven, and that he had accepted that his body could not go on any further. His joy was intact even though he was tired and weary. One of the last things he did was to write a letter to all of his optometry school classmates telling them of his cancer, and how he counted it all joy to have known them, and how he commended Jesus Christ as the one who cured his spiritual blindness and had given him vision to believe and know God. Bruce chose not to curse God or anyone else for having cancer, but he chose instead to bless others while having cancer. His days of playing trumpet brought joy to many, even while he battled cancer. His favorite songs to play for others were: "Victory in Jesus", "Shine Jesus Shine", and "Christ the Lord is Risen Today." His last words spoken were to his wife as he exclaimed what he saw: "Bright Light". Can you imagine a vision more fitting for an eye doctor to have at this bridge moment between earth and heaven? I think of the vision I had of Jesus, and the words "bright light" perfectly express both the glory of our Lord and the joy that He enlightens upon the pathway of our trusting souls. I believe that the glory of the Lord is what we shall behold in heaven as we see the face of Jesus our risen and glorious Savior. This same glory will be shining upon the face of God our loving Father. While there are troubles and trials upon the journey of life, there are far more joys and blessings that outweigh them all. Life is more than weighing the balance anyway, it involves following the path of righteousness and light, hope, truth and love.

On the night my brother Bruce Arnold died, I wrote down a poem entitled: "God's Silent Trumpets". That night was special because it was the day before Easter. I went in to the sanctuary at First Baptist Church of Battle Creek, Michigan where I was pastor, and I began to pray in the quiet stillness. It was the night before Easter. I looked around at the host of white lilies that were arranged on the altar, and I inhaled their sweet fragrance. Their open blooms reminded me of trumpets, each silently glorifying our risen Lord. I felt some grief as I realized that I would not hear my brother play "Christ the Lord is Risen Today" again on this earth. However, I could imagine hearing it with the beauty of suggestion offered by these vigilant and victorious lilies, God's silent trumpets. I shared the poem with the congregation on Easter Sunday, my sermon notes blessed with tears of joy and sorrow. Later that day we were together as family, and in a few days I read the poem at my brother's funeral. A month later, as I was praying at the church office, God gave me a melody to place with the words. Though my brother's passing was bittersweet, the testimony he left is still precious to family and friends. I believe that the witness of those who pass on may remain beautifully vibrant, though silent, like warm melodic tones played within our hearts. Our souls may listen to hear and rejoice in such clear trumpets of memory and feeling. I recall the time Bruce played Christmas carols with a brass ensemble on the downtown streets of Midland, Michigan for the Salvation Army. Bruce would raise his trumpet, finger the valves, and play so skillfully; there was no doubt that he did so to glorify God. Silent now, yet real within, is the sound of faith. Listen in your heart! Heaven's trumpets peal from the host who worship before God's throne.

God's Silent Trumpets

White and pure, bright and sure
Easter blossoms

A multitude of silent trumpets
Glorify the Risen Lord

The open lilies softly played
Their encore to the King

All children of God arose the joyfully sing.

Alleluia, alleluia, Christ the Lord is risen today
Alleluia, alleluia, Christ the Lord is risen today

Scott Arnold, 4-15-1995

9. Receiving a Peace that Prevails
(Bearing the blessing of peace)

When facing cancer and the overwhelming specter of treatments, most people try to find ways to cope with their anxiety and fears. Our common human will to preserve life and protect one another involves a built-in concern/fear of life-threatening illness, as well as a respectful concern for the unknown consequences of disease. These concerns/fears are faced through the ways that we help one another through the health care systems and support networks that we create. God gave us this potential and the gift of using our knowledge and abilities to help one another. In amazing ways, our bodies are designed to be worked on. While our health care systems have developed many methods of treating cancer, there is still much work to be done. While great advances have been made in understanding the origin and nature of cancer, there are still times when the cancer is too tough to beat, or too advanced to stop. Whether it is through health care, support systems, or through miraculous intervention, God is at work to give us the healing and peace that we need. The blessing of knowing the peace of Christ gives us assurance in His promise of "being with us always" (Matthew 28:20), no matter what we may face.

Looking back at the day when Thom was scheduled for radiation, there was something pivotal about that moment. From that experience the symbol of the cross is burned into my memory. The radiologist had taken a permanent black ink marker and had drawn a cross directly over the center of Thom's chest where the radiation was to take place. In this centralized location, directly over his heart and lungs, it was to me a sign of peace more than simply a technical marking. The cross of Jesus is to some a symbol of death and shame. Yet for those who believe Jesus did not die in vain, they believe that He reconciled us with God through His shed blood and then rose again three days later in victory over sin and death. For people of faith the cross symbolizes both death and life, a death to the sin that corrupts us and a life in the Spirit expressed through the power of Jesus' resurrection. How appropriate that a symbol of death and resurrection was placed above Thom's cancer. The cancer would need to be killed, but yet the peace of God was giving us hope that His life would endure.

Prevailing prayer was our ongoing practice in handling our crisis of cancer with Thom. To "pick up our cross" and follow Jesus required surrender, greater reliance upon His peace, and a belief in the Lord's working that surpassed our knowledge and understanding. We had to trust in the supernatural power of God to intervene. God placed the evidence and signs of support all around us. Then, God enlightened our dark and clouded understanding with brush strokes of intervention. In spite of the negative prognosis we had been given before he went in to the radiation room, we were willing to go forward because we believed in Jesus, our Prince of Peace. In that moment of miracle and revelation, the Spirit of God's peace prevailed. The type of cancer was clarified, no radiation was needed, and we were informed that the cure success rate of this chemotherapy was over 80%. The heavy burden upon our hearts was lifted. The wind of the Spirit blew fresh air into our souls. Much like people wait for the relief of a cool breeze on a hot humid day, our souls waited in longing and prayer for the winds of Heaven to breathe hope and healing. The day of heat and stagnation was now subsiding, giving way to the sweet relief of salvation. Peace came as we trusted and waited upon the working of God. When in the valley of the shadow of death, be assured, God is there. God is an ever present help in such times. Yes, God is able to deliver us!

King David received his training as a humble shepherd; he had learned to rely upon God in the midst of facing overwhelming foes, even giants. When facing cancer, believe in the power of God to bring it down through just a few stones flung in faith. As David wrote:

I will fear no evil, for you are with me;
your rod and your staff, they comfort me.
You prepare a table before me in the presence of my
enemies. You anoint my head with oil; my cup
overflows. Psalms 23:4-5 (NIV)

We may trust in the rod and staff of God, His sovereignty and His compassion. The Lord God is not only One who rules from above, but One who comes to us with His saving shepherd staff. The comforting presence and power of God is available to all who will repent of their sins and believe. When we repent we turn, away from sin and toward our redeemer. Though we may be surrounded by enemies of illness, various types of cancer or disease, God anoints our head with the oil of His gladness and healing. Even if our bodies are not healed, the center of our soul may be filled to overflowing. This is when the fruit of true and lasting peace is born within our souls.

The symbol of peace that we find in the cross helps us to recall that Jesus overcame evil with faith in His Father's love. He trusted the Heavenly Father's Sovereignty (the rod and staff) as He humbly absorbed our sin and brought forth a just means of salvation. The night before His crucifixion, Jesus had prepared a table of communion in the Passover feast; in His perfect offering of Himself he would defeat the enemies of sin and death. Though we did not deserve to be seated at the same table as God's Son, Jesus welcomed us. He adopted us. He even served us, washing our feet and anointing our heads with oil. He became the ultimate blood donor. To the cancer patient Jesus can be experienced through the help and sacrifice given by others. A blood transfusion reminds us not only of cleansing, but of restoration and new life.

When I think back to all of the ways that our Lord worked through nurses and doctors to bring comfort, support, and healing, my cup overflows with joy and peace.

The wonderful truth is that God uses people as signs, symbols, and vessels of His Kingdom of peace. Even though we might wonder at times if God is near, it only takes a moment of mercy by a caring nurse, doctor, or a medical technician to remind us that His ambassadors are surrounding us. On that critical day with Thom, we recount how God used the technician's marking of a cross, and a pathologist's diligence, to remind us that the cross is at the core of what it means to be a reconciled and redeemed people. Throughout our lives we are invited to trust that Christ is with us to give us peace and the assurance of protection. Our ultimate peace is the deliverance and power released through Jesus Christ's death and resurrection. Prior to His passion, after hours of explaining many things to His disciples, Jesus told them: *"In this world you will have trouble. But take heart! I have overcome the world."* John 16:33 (NIV) Jesus anticipated what He had to accomplish, and He knew He would need the peace of His Heavenly Father when He said *"Not my will, but Thy will be done."* Matthew 26:39.

In regard to the purpose for our lives, the Lord gives us peace to anticipate with faith what He will accomplish in and through us. The peace of God goes far beyond what we may understand at the present, because true peace is connected with the eternal. Any other form of temporary peace will eventually fail us. However, the solace of the Holy Spirit will faithfully minister to us with a steadfast love that endures forever. In fighting cancer, the peace of Christ is like good moist soil for the soul that helps us stay fresh in the fruit of the Spirit, even when death is before us.

When my grandfather, Rev. Forrest R. Gilmore, faced the realization in the winter of 1985 that he had only a few months to live because of a rapidly growing cancer, he talked earnestly with me. At that time Marilyn and I were newlyweds living near Boston, and he lived in Lynn, Massachusetts following his retirement from over 50 years as a Baptist minister. The first thing he affirmed was that he had peace with God through his faith in Jesus Christ. He wept, however, as he expressed his concern for his family. He was concerned about the salvation and welfare of his children and grandchildren. In the depth of his heart he was not concerned for himself, but asked that we pray for others. His passion was for his family to know the peace he had been blessed with. After he shared his hopes, vision, and wisdom with me, we both felt gratitude for sharing a relationship with Jesus Christ, and of having shared a calling to the Christian ministry. He then revealed his desires for his funeral service. He said: "I don't want this to be a service of mourning, but of celebration." Then he smiled and spoke gently, "Sing the hymns "Faith is the Victory" and "He Leadeth Me". He went on, "The service is to be a joyful coronation, a time to celebrate my homecoming in heaven." Weeks later, the Lord brought him home, and in the service we sang the peaceful and powerful hymns he requested. In looking at the words now, I see how powerful the message is for those who are facing cancer, and to those who are caregivers, as well as for those who are dealing with death or loss.

"He Leadeth Me" by Joseph Gilmore, 1862

He leadeth me, O blessèd thought!
O words with heav'nly comfort fraught!
Whate'er I do, where'er I be
Still 'tis God's hand that leadeth me.

Refrain:

He leadeth me, He leadeth me,
By His own hand He leadeth me;

His faithful follower I would be,
For by His hand He leadeth me.

Sometimes mid scenes of deepest gloom,
Sometimes where Eden's bowers bloom,
By waters still, over troubled sea,
Still 'tis His hand that leadeth me.

(Refrain)

Lord, I would place my hand in Thine,
Nor ever murmur nor repine;
Content, whatever lot I see,
Since 'tis my God that leadeth me.

(Refrain)

And when my task on earth is done,
When by Thy grace the vict'ry's won,
E'en death's cold wave I will not flee,
Since God through Jordan leadeth me.

The story of this hymn is all the more pertinent to how faith in the Lord leads us through life's battles. We find peace as we go forward with God's presence and leading. Joseph Gilmore shared the origin and development of the words of this hymn:

As a young man who recently had been graduated from Brown University and Newton Theological Institution, I was supplying for a couple of Sundays the pulpit of the First Baptist Church in Philadelphia [Pennsylvania]. At the mid-week service, on the 26th of March, 1862, I set out to give the people an exposition of the Twenty-third Psalm, which I had given before on three or four occasions, but this time I did not get further than the words "He Leadeth Me." Those words took hold of me as they had never done before, and I saw them in a significance and wondrous beauty of which I had never dreamed.

It was the darkest hour of the Civil War. I did not refer to that fact—that is, I don't think I did—but it may subconsciously have led me to realize that God's leadership is the one significant fact in human experience, that it makes no difference how we are led, or whither we are led, so long as we are sure God is leading us.

At the close of the meeting a few of us in the parlor of my host, good Deacon Wattson, kept on talking about the thought which I had emphasized; and then and there, on a blank page of the brief from which I had intended to speak, I penciled the hymn, talking and writing at the same time, then handed it to my wife and thought no more about it. She sent it to The Watchman and Reflector, a paper published in Boston, where it was first printed. I did not know until 1865 that my hymn had been set to music by William B. Bradbury. I went to Rochester [New York] to preach as a candidate before the Second Baptist Church. Going into their chapel on arrival in the city, I picked up a hymnal to see what they were singing, and opened it at my own hymn, "He Leadeth Me."

   - Joseph Gilmore 1862

   To know the peace of God that leads us is essential in the fight with cancer. We may not know anything else than His presence. We may not know if the chemotherapy or radiation will work. We may not know if cancer will return. We may not understand how we will find strength to carry on. We may not understand why a loved one has contracted cancer to begin with. We may not understand why cancer has come into our lives, or the life of a loved one. We may feel pain or go through suffering. Cancer may sweep over us like a cold wave, but we can be sure that "God through Jordan leadeth me." Through faith in Jesus Christ, our Savior and Prince of Peace, we can be sure of this: "He Leadeth Me".

Two months after my Grandfather Gilmore went to heaven, I was reading scripture in my office at the First Baptist Church of Needham, Massachusetts. In a moment of peace and quiet I felt the warmth of this beautiful Spring morning. It was one of those days when the tree blooms look like fine colored lace and the sky is as bright as an Irishman's eyes. I missed my grandfather and was thinking about him. At that moment our church bell carillon started to play the new hymns for the week. Providentially, God put it on the heart of the dear soul who arranged the hymns for that week to place "He Leadeth Me" as the first song. I knew without a doubt that God had arranged this and that my grandfather smiled down from heaven. In my inner-most being I was assured that God is faithful to lead and guide us. Most importantly, the truth of the Gospel that my grandfather lived to share with others was affirmed as clear as a bell within my soul. Jesus is the Savior and He is with us through faith, hope, and love. There is no greater peace and joy than to be led along the journey of life in a loving relationship with God through Jesus Christ.

10. Growing in Patience that Builds Character
(Bearing the blessing of patience)

Back when I was in college my church asked me to be a camp counselor for boys 11 to 13 years old. While some told me that the boys I was assigned to would be a handful, I discovered their willfulness and energy to be pure joy. We found vines over a hillside that overlooked "Bear Lake", and we would swing like Tarzan. We went on adventures, climbed trees, made awesome arts and crafts, talked about the first "Star Wars" movie, had a mouse make a nest in my sleeping bag, went fishing, and made up some fun alternative lyrics for the camp songs. Much to my surprise, the leaders decided to give me the "Patience of Job" award at the end. I am not sure why I deserved such an award, but many times since people have told me that I have great patience. Then again, perhaps they haven't seen me in traffic jams, and how I manage to initiate creative side routes. The blessing of patience is something that we may discover or appreciate in others, but honestly find lacking within ourselves. Going through a fight with cancer is probably one of the most challenging tests of patience.

In many years of ministry I have taught and preached about the fruit of God's Spirit. When I survey people about which fruit of the Spirit they need more of, the overwhelming answer is "patience". The fact is, patience is not inborn, it is learned. We grow to develop patience through character building experiences. None of us will find it a pleasant thing to be stretched, but when we are stretched, it can positively increase the development of patience if we look at it through the lens of faith. The Apostle Paul stated this insight very clearly to the persecuted Church of Rome when he wrote:

¹ Therefore, since we have been justified through faith, we have peace with God through our Lord Jesus Christ, ² through whom we have gained access by faith into this grace in which we now stand. And we rejoice in the hope of the glory of God. ³ Not only so, but we also rejoice in our sufferings, because we know that suffering produces perseverance; ⁴ perseverance, character; and character, hope. ⁵ And hope does not disappoint us, because God has poured out his love into our hearts by the Holy Spirit, whom he has given us.

Romans 5:1-5 (NIV)

Paul's insight was that God can use any experience we have in life for good, and ultimately the goodness of God's Glory and eternal Kingdom shall prevail within us as we overcome suffering and struggles through faith. Even our suffering can produce perseverance and courageous character. In life there is a process of refining going on. When one faces cancer and deals with emotional, mental, physical, financial, relational, and spiritual stress it is like being placed into a furnace. The belief that one can be refined and made more beautiful through this experience is often a reality that people discover.

A dear friend of mine, Carolyn Burnett, a retired elementary school teacher, once told me the story of how a little tea cup was made. The story goes something like this:

"One day a potter decided to make the most beautiful tea cup ever. Carefully the potter took the hard clay and worked on the clay until it was warm and soft. At first the clay complained, but soon the lump of clay realized it had become flexible in the potter's hands. As the tea cup took shape upon the potter's wheel, the lump of clay felt important, it had a new identity and purpose. The new tea cup sat beautifully upon the shelf. "I can hardly

wait to be used", thought the teacup. "Not yet", said the potter as he placed it in the hot furnace, "You need to be strengthened." The tea cup complained of the heat in the furnace, but soon it adjusted and felt stronger. The potter took the tea cup out and painted several beautiful colors of glaze on the tea cup. The tea cup felt special as the hands of the potter as it was set it down to dry. But again the potter placed the cup back in the hot furnace. Again the tea cup complained of the heat, but adjusted. When the tea cup came out it looked bright and colorful. "Now can I be used? Am I finished?" said the tea cup. "You still can become even more beautiful", said the potter. He took some white glaze and filled in more area. He placed the tea cup back in the oven at high heat. The tea cup complained some more, but was learning to trust the potter. Once again the tea cup came out, and looked even more splendid. "I must be finished now, said the tea cup." "Almost", said the potter. "You have one more round in the furnace to go." This time he painted on a clear glaze to make the tea cup shine even brighter. The tea cup went in and endured the heat with hope. Even though the tea cup thought that it would break each time it was in the furnace, the tea cup become even stronger as it was tempered and refined through the furnace. Now, when the tea cup came out it was the most beautiful and shiny piece that the potter had ever created. "Now you are finished, and I will use and cherish you always," said the potter. The tea cup smiled and thanked the potter for His love and patience."

If you have gone through battling cancer, or have been a supportive person to someone going through cancer treatments, then you can identify with the tea cup in the story. If you are a doctor, or a health care professional, then you can identify with the potter. The end result of going through the hot furnace of cancer treatments can be one of two things, either you will be refined or you will crack apart. When I speak of refinement or cracking, I am not referring to one's physical result, I am referring to one's character. A person can experience good results physically, but break apart emotionally, relationally, or spiritually. I know of several families who broke apart emotionally and relationally even though their loved one overcame the cancer and was healed. The experience can make you, or it can break you. There are stresses that are hard to endure; there are feelings that are difficult to manage. Going through cancer is like going through the furnace. Yet the potter knows that you have the potential to become stronger and brighter, even more beautiful.

Two friends and mentors of mine, Dr. Richard Schultheis and his wife Esther, evidenced great faith and godly character through their own battle with cancer. Esther had cancer as young mother, and through a number of years as a cancer survivor she was a radiant beam of love to many people. Then, later as her children were mostly grown up, her cancer returned. I didn't know that it had returned as she agreed to be one of our sponsors to stand at our wedding. Her son told me later, after the ceremony. I was amazed at her courage and grace, and we were all blessed by the peace that she emanated. During our wedding ceremony at North Shore Baptist Church of Chicago she came up with several others and made a commitment to watch over us and pray for us. I am sure that she is doing just that and more in heaven, patiently praying for us, committed to cheer us on to the finish line.

When I was battling cancer there were days when I was homebound and kind of loosing my mind. I pulled out a "3D Puzzle of the Eifel Tower of Paris" that I had found at a garage sale to build for my model electric train and car set. I had never done one of these puzzles before, so I took it out and began to figure out how to begin. It was overwhelming at first, and all the pieces looked quite a bit alike at first glance. The more I became familiar with it, the more the pieces started to become differentiated. I started by building the base, then the pillars of the tower, and the successive stages. There were many times that my patience was tested, but I persevered and eventually in about two weeks had a beautiful 40" tall, three dimensional, model of the famed "Eifel Tower". My family thought it was funny to see me work so hard on this puzzle. Perhaps the steroids had made me a little intense. Yet for me, doing this puzzle was a symbolic act that paralleled my own coming to terms with cancer. At first it is hard to know what to do, or how to make sense of this whole cancer thing. Step by step you work through it and eventually the pieces do come together. Persistence, perseverance, and prevailing patience are needed for the course of treatment.

Now there are some times when the pieces do not come together, and the puzzle remains just that, a puzzle. When this happens you need faith in the One who is able to put all things together in the right way. Without help people can often become dismayed, angry, and depressed. There are times that cancer is relentless. If our lives are being broken and shattered by it, there is intermediate help that comes from supportive community. Ultimate hope, however, comes only in the compassionate salvation of our loving God. If you are a person of faith who has cancer, but your family and friends can't understand or accept it, then your patience with them will be a testimony. If you are a person who struggles with faith and you have cancer, then perhaps cancer is more than an inconvenience, it may be a wake up call. God will allow us all to be tested, the question is, are we willing to be refined? Are we willing to be changed by grace within our souls?

When Thom was in the hospital, slowly gaining strength through what seemed like "endless numbered days", I felt inspired one night to write a song. I opened my computer and composed the following words, and that night put these thoughts to music.

In this Life

In this life there're be some trials
And some troubles too
God will always see you through
God's right hand is true
Trust His mercy that is always new

In this life I'll trust my Lord
And rely upon His Word
All together we shall praise His name
Gracious King and marvelous Lord
Come and worship sing with love and faith
Come and worship with your heart
Mighty God our hope is You through life
Mighty God our hope is You through pain
Merciful Savior come and glorify Yourself in our lives
Come and glorify Yourself in our lives

9-2005   Scott Arnold

The 2005 Arnold family: John, Marilyn, Thomas, Mark, Scott

11. Developing a Kindness that Touches Others
(Bearing the blessing of kindness)

Battles with cancer are often filled with peaks and valleys of emotion, discomfort, support, loneliness, hope, despair, miracles, struggles, anxiety and peace. These are just a few of the descriptive, yet insufficient, words that define the journey of having cancer, or of helping someone who has cancer. When you have gone through a significant 'mountain and valley' experience such as cancer, it can change how you treat others. For the most part people become kinder and gentler from battling cancer. Still, while I would like to say that surviving cancer always involves positive refinement. This would not be completely true for all survivors. Neither would it be true to say that only negative scars are left with those whose loved ones did not survive their battle with cancer. The fact is, cancer will change those who survive, those who were refined in their last days, or are surviving caregivers. People may become either kinder, or they may for a season or longer become bitter. I would like to believe that my experience of growing in kindness is shared by others whose empathy enlarged through the journey of facing death and dying. Yet I have observed that the difference between growing in either kindness or bitterness is frequently marked by the presence or lack of faith. When a person chooses to believe that there is a God who cares for them, and is with them in their need, and that God works through people they may trust, then that person will grow in experiencing the tender mercy and kindness of God. For some, though they survive and experience God's mercy, there may be an appreciation for life but a rejection of God. Gratitude for some is even difficult if they allow fear and anxiety to dominate their thinking toward the future. When cancer is approached without a strong trust in the tender mercy of God, anger can arise from one's sense of distress, frustration for lack of control, and hopelessness. It is difficult for someone who feels that their life is slipping from their hands, or is in some form of serious risk, to accept their limitations. Here is where God calls caregivers to exercise kindness and compassion. Family, friends, and even strangers will bless the cancer patient, caregiver, or survivor immensely.

Those who grow in kindness, including those who have overcome bitterness and despair, develop a depth of empathy. At hospitals and clinics personnel have the opportunity to give hope to cancer patients and their families with kindness. Likewise, cancer patients and their families have often shown kindness and appreciation to their caregivers. I remember how the nurses in Dr. Danish's clinic, and at the University of Michigan Hospital, were particularly skilled and kind in the way they administered chemotherapy. Through the focused medical attention given, and the power of personal concern that was expressed, God ministered to us. This was experienced in words, touch, and caring presence.

One of the greatest blessings came from my brother Paul and his family who lived near the hospital. He and his family faithfully visited, made their home available, brought us pizza or Chinese food, and made us feel loved. What a precious gift it is to have family! The visits from all of my family and Marilyn's family were a very powerful blessing. Kindness expressed from the heart of those who love us is often the greatest of gifts to reach our inner heart. We are then moved to accept and affirm that someone cares, and we are loved.

Once I was visiting a church member who was being prepared for a sensitive lung surgery at a world renowned Hospital. The family awaited his call to be brought in for preparation. As they brought him to the surgical prep area, a nurse came in and introduced herself rather quickly and abruptly. She asked the family and I to leave immediately while she prepared him for surgery. The tone of her voice was harsh, and the mood of the family and patient became tense. I asked her a question that I knew the answer to, but one that would clarify what would happen next: "Will we see him before he is brought to surgery so we can talk and pray with him?" "Well yes of course you will, don't be concerned, we just have to move quickly here because of all the surgeries we have today." We all walked out a bit ruffled and anxious. After about 20 minutes they called us back in, and as we asked about having a time to pray, this nurse said, "make it quick". Another nurse then walked in and said, "Hi, I'm Rose, I'll be your nurse from here to the operating room. Pray as long as you need to. We have time, and in fact you can walk with us up to the operating area."

Her kindness was a breath of fresh air. She said "Amen" with us at the end of the prayer. She spoke words of encouragement and hope as we wheeled down the hallway. The result was peace and joy in a moment when faith was being tested and life was on the line. When the family said goodbye to Frank prior to this delicate surgery, they were filled with hope because of the faith and the kind support and gentleness of the nurse. This woman reminded us of Della Reese in "Touched by an Angel". If you ever watched that television show you may recall how she and other angels were sent by God to help people in their times of stress and need. When the family was walking down the corridor of the hospital they remarked at what a blessing this nurse had been. His wife said: "It's as though God had sent an angel to minister to us." The family all agreed that the kindness of this nurse had made them and their husband/father feel at ease.

In what ways can we grow in kindness? Will others see a touch of heaven in our lives? We are not angels, but the Apostle Paul said that we can be ambassadors: *We are therefore Christ's ambassadors, as though God were making his appeal through us.* (2 Corinthians. 5:20 (NIV))

God shows His kindness through people. When people are not empowered by God's Spirit, they are drawing upon their own strength and resources. People may have good intentions and may show a level of kindness from themselves. However, the depth of kindness that we ultimately need, that we honestly long for, is found personally in a loving relationship with God. Such depth is needed when our patience is exhausted, and/or when our strength is depleted. Through faith we are empowered to be kind and loving to a degree that goes deeper and stronger than human willfulness alone. God's gift of grace works within one's soul for love. He resides in all who believe in Him, and thereby receive the Holy Spirit. You will need this in battling cancer, or in helping someone else to battle cancer. The battle is not pleasant; the call for sacrifice is often larger than you can handle well on your own. We need to be tapped into a strong connection with God. Jesus kindly calls us to trust in Him as our bedrock of truth and life. In Christ we may bear good fruit in life. We grow to rely upon His eternal love and steadfast care.

When people of faith show the kindness of God it is a sweet joy to all. However, when people lose their kind spirit, it is often because they have fallen back to their own resources, and feel threatened or afraid. There are also times when chemotherapy and physical weakness can affect a cancer patient's level of sensitivity and ability to handle stress. For example, medical steroids are certainly a helpful part of reducing the negative physical side effects of chemotherapy, but they also can trigger certain other physical and mental responses. Change of diet, lack of exercise, lack of sleep, change in social or work environments, are all additional factors that can affect one's peace of mind. All the more, these and other factors make battling cancer difficult and help us to understand how cancer patients and their caregivers need to find God as their greater source for peace, harmony, and wellness.

With regard to pain and discomfort, suffering is a reality that moves us to desire and appreciate kindness. The fruit of suffering endured often leads toward a kindness passed on to others. There is a sort of fellowship in suffering that leads people to depths of kindness and understanding. People of faith recognize the light of God's mercy and grace while facing adversity or struggles. The sharing of kindness leads people to empowerment that carries them through pain and fear. Kindness is like soothing oil to calm, heal, and give courage. Kind words are precious gifts to endear hope. Kind actions are like sweet bread, whose fiber is faith, whose reception is like love that is blessed and broken, a gift from heaven.

I have been in many nursing homes and hospitals where kindness is the difference between a cold and sterile environment and an environment of love and support. At the heart of kindness there is a respect for people. The conscience of kindness believes that serving one another is precious, a sacramental service. Kindness does not always come easy; in a hospital/care setting it is often given by those who are willing to stoop low to take extra measures to keep patients clean, comfortable, healthy and happy. Kindness implies more than just a minimal level of care; it involves an inspired type of care. Kindness is treating people with extraordinary care, for it involves special attention, extra effort, intentionality, and unconditional love. Genuine kindness grows out of the inner character of love that God cultivates in us, and calls us to bless others with. Think of kindness for a few minutes. After some thoughtful reflection you will soon picture the face of someone who has been a faithful and true friend.

The Face of a True Friend

Tired and feeling frail
Cancer and treatments sap me dry
I need attention, a helping hand
I thirst for compassion, the face of a friend

Patience is wearing thin
Strength and resolve are low
I call out, a helping heart
I desire kindness, a touch of grace

Kindness answers in a smile
A voice cheers and serves to inspire
I am touched with kind hands and heart
I have beheld the face of a true friend

-Scott Arnold 2006

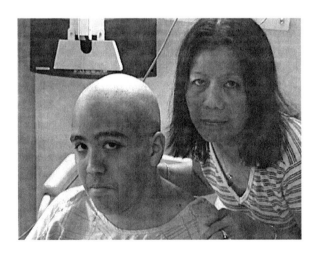

Marilyn and Thom at Mott Children's Hospital.

12. Greeting Life in View of God's Goodness
(Bearing the blessing of goodness)

When a person is facing cancer or another life-threatening illness, they will re-evaluate life. Though people may have a mix of emotions and thoughts, for most there will be an increased awareness of the goodness of life. This awareness may be a bright epiphany for some, and for others it may be a heightened awareness. For me, cancer renewed a child-like trust in God. I affirmed and rediscovered the goodness of God in simple blessings. I found that I was more interested in people, realizing that all of us have a limited time on this earth. Because of this we need to appreciate one another more. We may notice more of the intrinsic value of the soul, and the interesting facets of personality expressed uniquely by others. Though my family may have found it annoying, I would take time to listen intently, and study my wife and sons with curious interest and fascination. I came to a greater appreciation of their unique qualities and talents. I also came to a greater unconditional love of myself and others, accepting myself and others as frail human beings who have true hope in the grace and goodness of God.

Through all this observation, I came to the conclusion that we could dwell on our imperfections, or we could trust in the one who is at work to perfect us. We could dwell on the cancer, or we could rely upon the one who is at work to heal us and help us overcome. We could be obsessed with death, or we could live our lives with faith, hope, and love. If we choose to trust in the goodness and grace of God, and secure a loving relationship with Jesus our redeemer, there is nothing that will separate us from our Heavenly Father. Praise God for His mercy! Praise God from whom all blessings flow!

When our son Thom was released from the University of Michigan Hospital for his first respite between cancer treatments, we decided to go on a simple "safe" fun trip. We went a few hours away to see an African Lion and Game Safari near Hamilton, Ontario. We drove through one area where there were cheetahs, another with lions, and then we came to the baboons. They jumped on to every vehicle that came through and looked at us through the windows. One of the young baboons used the side mirror of our car to groom himself. It was a sight to see all these hairy clowns ride and jump around from vehicle to vehicle. There is no question that God made monkeys to remind us of how fun life can be. Later, in another area, several giraffes came up, stuck out their long tongues, and put their faces up to the window. After lunch at the compound, we heard the announcement of the "Elephant Parade", and we watched 12 elephants walk to the pond together single-file, trunks holding tails. They went in and started splashing around, blowing water over their shoulders and at one another. As we left, Thom and his brothers all agreed that we had enjoyed a great time together. This was a time of laughter and light-hearted goodness. Families need good times shared together to create positive memories, and promote family unity.

While we had been in the park, my mother had called me from Michigan, and told me that dad and her were in the hospital in Midland. They had just come down from up north earlier because of how dad was feeling, and now he was in the emergency room. When she told my dad what we were doing, he smiled and told her "that's just like Scott, finding a way to have fun". An hour later, when we had just left the park, my brother Paul called and told me that dad was in serious condition, and needed to be brought to another hospital where they could run more tests. He told me: "They are saying that there are indications of an acute cancer and that his blood counts are extremely unhealthy. Come as soon as you can." We went directly home, and soon I arrived at St. Mary's Hospital in Saginaw, Michigan. The doctor explained to us in a very caring and direct way that dad had a type of cancer that grows rapidly in the blood stream, often undetected. His vital organs were starting to close down, and there was nothing that could be done about it at this point. In fact, the doctor indicated that he may not live more than another day. The decision to hook him up to life and breath support, and try to keep him alive, was already upon us. He was weak and could say very little, yet what were we to do? If we chose to avoid life support for the sake of having a little more time to talk with him, we might risk some slim chance of hope for a clearer picture and diagnosis, along with possible treatment. As it was, we chose life support because the diagnosis was still partly inconclusive. At first, as he perked up with breath support, it was clear that he wanted to speak and talk, but could not with the tube. He made direct eye contact with us all, and with his hands gestured that he loved us. In bittersweet tears we affirmed his message and told him that we loved him. I let him know that he had always been faithful to tell us in words how much he loved us and that we understood. Each of us in our own way were trying to deal with our grief while saying good bye. I remember praying with him and entrusting him into the care of Jesus Christ our Lord and Savior.

As we continued to communicate our love to him, he heard us and nodded with affirmation, with his blue eyes and hands he tried to find a way to express all the deep feelings he had for us. My mind flashed back to the previous Thanksgiving and at other family gatherings of late in which he had said: "In case I die, you should know how blessed I am to have a wife like Esther, and children and grandchildren like all of you. I am so blessed and proud." Now here he was, with little notice or symptoms, dying of cancer, and there was nothing we could do about it but accept God's timing. Maurice Gene Arnold was blessed, and he made a point of helping others unselfishly. The way he lived embodied "goodness", "joy" and "faith". He quickly and gently moved into the next life, only 24 hours from the time he went into the hospital. It was a type of Leukemia that quickly attacked and gave us little or no time to know how to respond. Even so, we had to accept what had taken place. We came to trust and believe that God knew what He was doing in taking our father home to heaven at that time. Though we felt genuine and deep grief and loss, I believe that his Lord and Savior Jesus was glad to receive him and say: "Well done, good and faithful servant. Receive your reward in heaven. Come and be with me in my Father's house that I have prepared for you."

Many people came to the visitation at the funeral home, and they shared story after story of his unselfish kindness and service. One man came representing Eagle Village, a home for children and teens who are being emotionally and socially rehabilitated. He told us of how Gene helped them raise many thousands of dollars to build housing and other buildings for their village. Another man told us of how Gene had worked with others in the creation of a downtown senior housing complex and a number of other community improvements in Midland, Michigan. Still another man came and told us of how our father had been instrumental in improving race relations at the college and in the community. Person after person had a story or two to tell, and each added to the witness of how one person can be a blessing of good will and a light of hope. This was a wonderful affirmation of the impact he had made in the community. We marveled because our perspective was more intimate. We knew a father who was loving, fun, helpful, kind, and compassionate. They knew a man who was an organizer, encourager and helper in the community; one who looked for the good in others and cultivated good-will. The funeral service at the Memorial Presbyterian Church helped us to affirm and express the importance of our shared faith in God. My sister Nancy, and my brother Paul and I, were all able to share in father's eulogy. We expressed our gratitude to God for dad, and we were able to express the faith we hold true that Jesus Christ is Savior and Lord. We not only celebrated dad's life, but we also celebrated his faith and ours. We believe that Jesus died and rose again, and that there is nothing that can separate us from the love of God in Christ Jesus our Lord. We affirmed that when Jesus rose again and ascended to heaven, he did so in order to prepare the way to heaven for those who believe in Him. This was not the end for Gene Arnold's soul, as if cancer was a thief that could take our father away from our hearts, or take our hope of heaven away. We affirmed that God had blessed us all with a great person, and that his time on earth had come to an end. We looked forward to a future time, a time of God's transforming reign and manifested Kingdom beyond our limited sight and temporary loss. With grateful hearts, God had blessed our souls with the comfort of His promise that some day we shall see our Savior face to face, and our father, brother, family and friends in Heaven as well.

Months and years later, we have been able to look back and see more clearly that God was with us to help us then. He ushered dad into the Eternal Kingdom without much suffering. There have been tears of love shed in our loss and memories, and this is healthy, right, and natural. Love that is felt deeply must express itself. Faith grows ever stronger. Through this, the promise and hope of heaven has grown to be bright and secure in our hearts and minds. God taught us once again about the fragile nature of this life, and how we were blessed with the testimony of faith and goodness that our dad had given us. Once again we affirmed that we must cherish and value one another and "praise God from whom all blessings flow". God gives us faith and hope to overcome cancer and death's sting.

As you may recall, my father's death happened while Thom was in the midst of his battle with cancer. Dad had been quite concerned for Thom. There was no question that he was in deep prayer for the healing of his grandson, and in visiting him at the hospital he told Thom to "keep the faith". For all of us, dad's life and faith had been both encouraging and inspiring. For Thom, he became even more aware of the threat that cancer posed. He expressed this several years later as he recalled how his grandfather's death made him all the more determined to fight and win the battle he was facing with cancer. Thom grew to realize that he was surrounded by caring family and friends, but also most importantly that God would be his ever present help, strength, and hope.

One of the lasting memories and legacies shared by my father was his love of growing and giving roses from his garden. If anyone strolled past his garden on the sidewalk nearby, they could not only see his roses but also pause to appreciate their inviting fragrance. Dad would regularly surprise people by presenting them with carefully cut roses, their colorful petals touching many a heart. Dad made it a priority to bring freshly cut roses right in to mom along with a kiss. The bright blooms were promptly put in a crystal vase and placed gratefully by mom on the dining room table. The key expressions of Dad were that of joy, love, and generosity, given to family, friends, and even strangers. The rose for us has been a flower that carries great meaning, and in some miraculous way can even bear beautiful "soul fruit" for the giver and receiver alike.

The Goodness of a Rose's Bloom

The goodness of a rose's bloom
Sweet fragrance and colorful delight
T'was not detectable in winter's doom
Nor seen in early spring's fragile light

Goodness was yet there all along
Even the thorns could not hide
Beauty that inspired a fresh song
Grace that is bright, beautiful and wide

The goodness of a rose's bloom
Sweet fragrance and colorful delight
T'is radiant life over the tomb
A corsage of love from my Savior bright

Scott Arnold
2008

13. Leaning upon Divine Faithfulness
(Setbacks provide further steps toward spiritual growth)

What is divine faithfulness? How can one learn to trust in God through those times of trial or setback that test our faith? This is a big issue when medical test results for a cancer patient offer little or no hope. When treatment weakens you, or when limitations make it frustrating to function or cope, divine faithfulness is the one ultimately stable foundation to rely upon. The fact that people seek answers to the great mysteries and challenges of life is, in itself, a testimony to the wonder that spiritually we are made in God's image. Even so, the attribute of weakness for people in crisis is not the only thing that compels them to seek and discover God's grace and love. The potential of a profound leap of faith is based upon people perceiving a glimpse of our Creator's enduring presence and eternal power, even while in the midst of illness, pain, or suffering. God is constantly revealing something of His nature and presence. Going through cancer or other challenges in life will make us more vulnerable, which if approached with faith, will give us eyes to see and ears to hear. We may even discover that our hearts and minds become more accessible to our faithful Creator's spiritual reality and redemptive work.

God is with us in the battle with cancer. God works through the faithfulness of family, friends, doctors, and nurses. Yet we wonder how far we can be stretched as we battle cancer. An encouraging, life-affirming, ray of hope is needed. Trusting God's faithfulness is essential in those moments when we must face death and the acceptance of our temporary mortal state. To look beyond our existence in these bodies is to believe in a life that is transcendent and even transforming of our current temporary realm. God is faithful to minister to us each day, but even more so, God's faithfulness is eternal. God is working out His plan of salvation and transformation for those who believe and receive His gift of grace, this being administered through His Son Jesus Christ.

God answers people through a variety of interventions and provisions; all this as participatory prayers are lifted up. God will work through the treatments, tests, and trials we go through. People led by God's Spirit are often the divine instruments of faithfulness and intervention. Though we may not see God directly, we may grow to see God activating and directing the relationships, events, and connections made from day to day. The vitality of our faith is related to our vision of faith in response to the ways that God is already at work.

Time after time God has faithfully worked through people to provide care. Sometimes a specific doctor or nurse provided encouragement and intervention; other times it was another patient or caregiver. There was one time when we were wondering how we could pay for Thom's treatments and hospitalization. Then we met another parent of a fellow cancer patient who told us about our state's "Children's Special Health Care Services" supplemental insurance program. This turned out to be a tremendous blessing and answer to prayer. We should not be surprised that when we pray God works to answer us and provide according to specific needs and concerns. Timing is critical when it comes to intervention and care, and the hand of God has been unmistakable in the midst of hospitalization and treatments. In so many ways, looking back, we can see God's faithfulness through the assistance of others.

In the midst of all this seriousness I am compelled to share a few light-hearted stories about a wonderful addition to our family. Three months into Thom's nine month intensive fight with cancer he begged for a dog. Since he had always wanted to have a dog, we decided that it may be an encouragement and healthy distraction. The plan was to have a dog in mind for him to see as he returned home. So before Thom came home, his brother John and I went to the humane society with the goal of finding a cute and happy dog. One of the first dogs I noticed was a white medium-sized poodle mix whose name was "Sugar". She immediately connected with me through eye contact. We went around several times to look at all the other dogs, but we came back to this yellow-eyed, shaggy white dog. The information card told us that her owner had become ill, and this was why she needed a home. Marilyn and Thom met us at the humane society as we were making our choice. Thom also liked "Sugar". As I filled out the paperwork while looking at this dog, I wondered what kind of an adventure we were getting ourselves into.

"Sugar" turned out to be a great dog. At first she was quiet and somewhat reserved. We had much to learn, and I think she may have known this. Since she was quite shaggy it was clear she needed a bath, so on the second day we brought her for a shampoo and hair cut. She looked sad as we left her, but when we returned she was so glad to see us that she let out her first bark, it sounded like a howl of joy. It was as though she was telling the world "Here is my family, I am loved." Sugar has taught us the importance of going out for walks, taking time to relax, and the blessing of faithfulness. Yes, she has been a faithful friend, coming alongside us for companionship and empathy. She is always joyful to greet us, and always ready to defend family and home. She follows us around, and helps us to smile and laugh. One time I came home to notice that she was rolling around in the dirt of the backyard. Immediately a familiar odor permeated my senses, she had been skunked! She wanted to go back into the house, but an outdoor bath was in order. It took 5 baths, tomato juice, and four weeks of airing out for the skunk odor to dissipate. Her bout with the skunk, and our sacrificial love to help her, reminded me of the kind of commitment and care it takes while dealing with cancer. While cancer truly stinks, our commitment to serve and our long-suffering to bear with one another faithfully makes a difference.

Maintaining a clear vision of God's faithfulness is challenging in that cancer patients and their families must deal with immediate and ongoing physical and emotional struggles. Furthermore, there are concerns that weigh strongly about future unknown variables that can stir up anxiety. Sometimes our faith is strong, other times our faith is weak. But the key factor is not how strong or weak we are, but how true and faithful God is. Our approach to God, therefore, needs to be humble and open. Jesus told a parable of two men who went to the temple to pray. One was boastful and filled with self-righteousness, the other was humble and filled with repentance before God. One relied upon his own standard of spirituality, and the other relied upon God's standard of spirituality. One relied upon his own strength, the other relied upon God's strength. One trusted in his own attributes, the other trusted in the attributes of the one who created him. One saw hope in himself, the other saw hope as being beyond himself. One fought the cancer of the soul with denial, the other fought the cancer of the soul with trust in God and His grace. Can you guess who left the temple blessed by the Spirit of God?

God is faithful to help us learn through illness, trial, and temptation. When we acknowledge our need for help, it is not a sign of weakness but of faith in the one who is always faithful. Prayer is the primary agency of relying upon God. The problem is that many people are not honest with themselves as they pray. If the standard of comparison we use is our own definition of health or goodness, then we are bound to compare ourselves simply to others and not to God's definition of health or goodness. In this respect a person can appear to be healthy outwardly, but not be healthy inwardly, spiritually. Likewise, a person can be unhealthy physically, but be healthy inwardly, spiritually. Our whole condition, spiritual, emotional, mental, social, relational and physical is important to God. If we humble ourselves to accept our need for help we will find that God is faithful to intervene, encourage, inspire and reveal. The first step for each of us is confession and honesty before our holy and gracious Lord, the Great Physician. God's faithfulness can not be measured according to either good health or bad health, but is simply a gift through all times to people who believe. They who believe shall receive God's all-sufficient grace through each and every condition of life, including difficult health conditions.

Recently I went to visit Nancy B., a dear member of our church, at a hospital an hour away from home. After I had visited and prayed with her before she went for surgery, I had an hour to do an errand. As I drove a short distance I noticed a very strong smell of gasoline. I popped open the hood of the 20 year old 1988 BMW, and noticed a pin hole leak springing out from a rubber hose above the engine cylinders. The gasoline evaporated on the hot engine each time it squirted out. In that moment it occurred to me that this might be dangerous, it could catch on fire. So I left the hood open for the engine to cool down. I realized how fortunate I was that I caught this now, and had not ignored the warning signs of the smell. I was thankful that our 16 year old son was not driving when this occurred, he probably would not have known what to do. Visions of scrambling out of a car potentially going up in flames helped me realize how important it was that I did not deny the symptoms that warned me of an underlying problem. This is likewise true with cancer detection, prevention, and early diagnosis. Applied to spiritual matters, alertness can also prevent us from being burnt by an underlying problem in one's soul. Fuel in the right direction gives energy and purpose, fuel in the wrong place can be explosive and destructive.

After identifying the problem, I went back into the hospital waiting room and met Nancy's son Joe who had

107

just arrived. He and I were able to go back outside and fix the problem by cutting and reattaching the hose. There was just enough extra hose to spare. The more important part was that Nancy's surgery went well, and so, incidentally, did the little surgery on the car too.

When you go through the journey of cancer personally, or with someone you love, there is hope that it will involve a cure, or at least some degree of physical healing. The process of fighting cancer, or of being supportive to those in the fight, develops the character qualities of vigilance and faithfulness. Our family has many memories of going through the struggle that Thom and I faced with cancer. Thom's battle was considerably more difficult and life threatening. Had I not faced cancer before, I don't think I would have been as prepared to deal with Thom's battle. Even then, how do you prepare for something so intense? How can you know about the challenges that will come? The preparation we need is internal and external, both spiritual and relational. A vital connection with God and others brings health and hope.

One scripture passage that reminds us that God is faithful to complete the good work that He begins in our lives was written by the Apostle Paul:

I thank my God every time I remember you. In all my prayers for all of you, I always pray with joy because of your partnership in the gospel from the first day until now, being confident of this, that he who began a good work in you will carry it on to completion until the day of Christ Jesus. Philippians 1:3-6 (NIV)

This passage of promise is a great comfort for those who wonder if they will be able to complete the things in life that cancer is making difficult or impossible to accomplish. It does not say that we will accomplish all the things that we deem important, but that Christ will complete those things in our lives that are essential to His good work and gracious will. I sometimes catch myself, even now as a six year cancer survivor, wondering how many more years God will grant me. For a moment, a day, or even a week or longer, I have found myself trying to accomplish too much of what I want, and not necessarily those things that God would want. So often, if we are honest, we focus on what we think we should accomplish and not necessarily upon what God wants to accomplish in and through us. Sometimes, even if we hope to accomplish great things for God, we can misunderstand the will of God to be achievement oriented and not relationship or character oriented. The goal of doing God's will should arise from being a person of God. In the face of adversity we might lose sight of the objective of God, who is allowing us cancer for a reason. The truth is, we are allowed cancer to bring us nearer to God so that spiritual (soul) fruit may be developed. Through receiving the refinement of God to develop our character, a great measure of grace that we receive shall bear a good work of sanctifying holiness.

The essential blessings that cancer offers survivors are twofold: recognition of our limitations and also an awareness of God's near presence. Both of these areas of blessing do not limit God, but acknowledge His unlimited potential within our weakness or limitations. We all want to accomplish something significant and purposeful in and through our lives. But when cancer comes into the picture we suddenly realize that we were not in as much control as we thought we were. In the midst of our adjustments, and our acceptance of limitations, God promises to extend His grace and goodness through our faith in Jesus Christ and through our reception of God's Holy Spirit. This comes about through surrendered belief. God is ever present. He calls us into a personal relationship, a redeeming friendship through His Son Jesus. Likewise He calls us to be true friends with one another, supporting each other, especially through the battle with cancer. Caring friends are one of life's greatest gifts, for they cheer us on to victory.

Faithful Friend

Friend, faithful and free
Have a seat, stay with me
For I feel weak and tired

Friend, listen and hear
Draw your head near
For I need to affirm your love

Friend, reach and touch
Place your hand as such
For in your presence I am blessed

Scott Arnold
10-31-2008

Scott and Thom at their first relay for life in 2006

14. Going about Life with Gentleness
(Becoming an agent of mercy and compassion)

When someone goes through a life-threatening illness, one positive outcome can be a stronger sense of mercy and compassion for others. The outward expression of gentleness is the fruit of God's spirit that comes through weathering adversity. When one's worldview is shaped by a deeper sense of God's mercy it will sensitize that person toward increased empathy and awareness of others' needs. The words you speak and the gestures that accompany your actions are more closely monitored and measured. Spiritual maturity develops for many who fight cancer from this depth of caring. In addition, through the counsel of the Holy Spirit of God, there is a heightened awareness of purpose that will lead to responsive action. For the sake of the Kingdom of God on earth, what we say and what we do will have a lasting impact on those we care for. Within one's soul the fruit of dealing with cancer can bring a softening that is born of suffering, a perceptive peace that prevails over pain and a responsive growth that comes by faith. The mercy of God is received into the hearts of those who hunger for grace and redemption.

Parents of kids with cancer understand that there are specific instances when added acts of mercy offer encouragement to their children. Thom was hospitalized a few days before turning 16 years old, just before he was about to be a licensed driver in the state of Michigan. Four months after, at a time when he could drive again, we surprised him by giving him the car of his dreams. He had been looking online at old '1960's"orange Volkswagen Beetles. We found a 1968 bright orange Beetle with a white interior. Thom was thrilled and overjoyed when I drove it home for him. He promptly named the car "Rita". The inspiration for the name came from the "Beatles" song "Lovely Rita, Meter Maid". This happy and fun car made children stop, point, have their parents look, and then smile back to us in return. People would wave and comment through their opened car windows at red traffic lights. Thom soaked it all in, and enjoyed the whirl of the engine and putting his hand out to sculpt the breeze. On his first day back to school months later, he was noticed as he made a bright and cheerful entrance. Thom felt good about life and the "soul fruit" in his life that had increased. He went on that year to grow in faith and friendship mainly because he learned to approach others with a greater sense of appreciation and compassion.

There are simple, yet profound, lessons that God has taught me in practicing the art of being gentle and caring for others. One time when our church had scheduled a trip to an amusement park it was unclear how many people would be able to go. It turned out that we had seven people who could go, much fewer than we had first anticipated. I wondered if it was worth it, but decided I must maintain my promise and commitment. We ended up having a great time on a beautiful day. One of the persons who came as an additional participant with our group that day was a guy named Derrick. Derrick was in his late 20's and he had a severe bicycle accident when he was in high school; this has left Derrick challenged mentally and physically. Outwardly, his face and hesitant speech would lead people to think that he is retarded, but he is not. He is quite smart, and though awkward physically and socially, he is quite capable. What Derrick appreciates is when people can understand and accept him as he is. During our time at "Michigan's Adventure" Derrick and I went on a few of the water rides together. At first he was reluctant to go down some of the slides, but gradually he built up courage. Then we looked over to the "mother of all water rides" at the park: "The Funnel of Fear". He wasn't so sure about going on it at my first suggestion, but I convinced him that we could do it. Throughout the wait in line, as we rolled the big round raft up the ramp, he kept asking me if it was going to be alright. I kept boosting his confidence with words of encouragement. Near the top of the funnel we could watch others go down the swift current of an enclosed long tube into a giant funnel that swept up and around and down through an opening into descending rapids and a finishing pool. I could see he looked anxious as he laughed nervously. I had to admit that I too was also a little bit anxious. However, by faith we stepped up to the loading pool, and flopped onto the raft. I realized as the raft loader secured us that I was going to be sitting up backwards going down. With one quick push we were soon rapidly descending a long dark steep tunnel. We both held on and yelled the whole way down. It was a blast! Down through the dark twisting maze, holding on, the light broke through as we swished down and then up quickly on the high wall of the big funnel of fear. In this moment we looked at each other with a mix of surprise, joy, and thrilled courage. The raft then reached it's apex in the funnel and we swung down again, and then up again, down and up one more time as we spiraled through the funnel into the finish line of rushing, foaming, water. We laughed and yelled with hearty joy as we concluded this shared experience of relying upon our faith to overcome fear. After we came to a stop I got out and reached out to help him up out of the raft. He took my hand and then after he stood up, we gave each other a big hug and Derrick looked at me with a sense of accomplishment as he said: "We did it! That was cool man!" It was a beautiful moment. As I retrieved the raft I looked over to the crowd of people waiting their turn and saw that all had been watching us. They could see that Derrick was not your "normal" person, but the expression I saw was that of shared joy and respect on their part, a sense of participating in his moment of triumph. Deep in my heart, in that moment, I reflected on the fact that I almost didn't come to the park that day. I realized that if I had not, I would have missed this bright moment of blessing. When I share this story I am reminded that faith requires compassion and gentleness. You won't know the blessing of sharing this until after you go through the dark tunnels and perilous waters. Eventually you do come through and there is a host who will welcome you and be blessed at your courage and arrival.

God provides people who can understand, accompany, and intervene to help when we struggle and battle with cancer. There will be "funnels of fear" that we go through. The presence and support of others is vital to maintain courage. God provides people to be His agents of mercy and compassion. Sometimes God surprises the world by working through the weak, the heavy laden, the cancer fighters, the survivors, and the caregivers who have learned to tap into the support of God's Spirit. God has given each person the potential for expressing mercy and gentleness. We need faith in order to reach God's gracious level of acceptance and empathy. Jesus calls us to grow in stepping forward to care for others. Consistently this means being gentle, truthful, courageous, and forgiving. Jesus spoke to His disciples saying:

So watch yourselves. "If your brother sins, rebuke him, and if he repents, forgive him. If he sins against you seven times in a day, and seven times comes back to you and says, 'I repent,' forgive him." The apostles said to the Lord, "Increase our faith!"   Luke 17:3-5 (NIV)

The Lord has made it clear that to be His disciples we must express God's mercy with patience, gentleness, and consistency. This requires increased faith in the one who has the power to transform lives, and with this, the power to forgive and heal. Those who are battling severe illness, cancer, or life-threatening options, can sometimes be angry and cantankerous. They need our sympathy and gentleness, forgiveness and grace, and sometimes our tough love. Those who are caring for their loved ones who are undergoing treatment or troubles with cancer also need our

114

respectful support. When people react to our kindness by venting their stress or by being verbally explosive, God's forgiveness and grace must be extended through our listening/caring presence. The fact is, the struggle with cancer can be overwhelming, and it takes extra mercy for all involved. That's why Jesus taught His disciples to forgive over and over again. You never know when it will be you in that moment of weakness and struggle. Because of God's enduring love, and the compassion and mercy of others, we come to appreciate how "amazing" grace is. God can use cancer to teach us to place more emphasis on forgiveness than upon our failings or fears. God is patient and gentle in the way that His Spirit moves. Therefore, may we not miss the opportunity to know and share the gentle love of God with one another.

15. Suffering that Builds Self-Control
(Living within limits and pain)

Why is there suffering? People have debated and deliberated on the purpose of pain. On a physical level pain is understandable as the sensory detection we are given when something is not right, is broken, or is in need of attention. Suffering involves the spectrum of difficulties that we experience as we live with pain and the limits of our physical existence. Short-term suffering is often seen as acceptable and in some cases necessary to achieve a greater gain; whereas long-term suffering is often misperceived as unacceptable and a possible sign of divine punishment. Suffering can have a purpose, and in many situations can be turned toward constructive ends. In either short or long term situations, suffering involves dealing with the limits of our bodies and the reality of our mortality. Our bodies are not made to live forever. Our bodies are corruptible, imperfect, and subject to decay. Because all of us will die, and will meet our maker, it is essential that we learn to develop ways to cope with pain and suffering so as to make the most of the life we are given. We may find blessings in the midst of every aspect of life. Through suffering we learn to accept our boundaries, and to trust in God who has no boundaries. Through suffering we learn to draw upon greater resources for strength and support.

New life, or renewal of hope, is often discovered through our personal battles and our shared suffering. In teaching his disciples about his upcoming sacrifice on the cross, Jesus spoke about God's impending work of mercy that would become possible through His perfect sacrifice on the cross:

"The hour has come for the Son of Man to be glorified. I tell you the truth, unless a kernel of wheat falls to the

ground and dies, it remains only a single seed. But if it dies, it produces many seeds. John 12:23-24 (NIV)

When a person learns the art of self-control through suffering, it will result in accepting one's situation as it may benefit others as well as oneself. How is this so? From the witness of faith in life's times of suffering one may identify with the need for salvation, and through identification with Christ's suffering, one is able to find courage. Those who see the faith and strength of the suffering person will say to themselves, "If they can believe in the midst of their suffering, and bless the Lord, and bless others; then I want to know and believe in the God they are experiencing." The fact that Jesus blessed people and did not curse those who persecuted and crucified Him tells us something about how suffering can be turned around for good.

Jesus also shows us through the cross how powerful God's love and forgiveness can be when we exercise self-control. Jesus accepted, even embraced, the limits of being human, when in fact He was also fully divine. Jesus glorified God by taking upon Himself all of our sin on the cross. In so doing He not only justified and forgave us, He also defeated the principalities of evil and the powers of sin for our salvation. Three days later He rose from the dead. Jesus triumphed over evil and secured victory for all who believe. Jesus Christ, the single perfect divine seed of God, was sent to earth, had fallen to the ground and had died. In the power of the resurrection, this seed arose to bloom and produce many seeds that would grow within the hearts of all who would come to life by saving faith. The offer of grace, forgiveness, and eternal life that is born of God's Spirit is available to any one who will believe and receive Jesus Christ as Savior and Lord.

I have known and counseled people who have struggled with the suffering and limits of cancer. One person came and told me how they were ready to leave their spouse and family for a while. It was all just too difficult, and they did not feel supported. The first thing I did was to just listen and allow the person to keep talking. Eventually the larger issue came out, "I am struggling with my faith. I just wonder what God is doing in the midst of all of this?" This person felt that they had reached their limit, and they wanted assurance that they were not alone or abandoned by God. Sometimes when a person feels abandoned and alone it is their own projection of fear and anxiety. This can become pronounced when a person is in the midst of dealing with mortality, or their limitations and pain. The choice given to those in the midst of suffering is to either believe or doubt the presence and power of God. The temptation the Devil throws at us in the crisis of pain is to doubt God's existence. Yet it is the existence of pain itself that could also draw us to the source of healing, physically, emotionally, and spiritually. The Apostle Paul wrote his letter to the church in Rome, fully aware that they were suffering for the sake of the gospel seed of Jesus Christ.

> *Therefore, since we have been justified through faith, we have peace with God through our Lord Jesus Christ, through whom we have gained access by faith into this grace in which we now stand. And we rejoice in the hope of the glory of God. Not only so, but we also rejoice in our sufferings, because we know that suffering produces perseverance; perseverance, character; and character, hope. And hope does not disappoint us, because God has poured out his love into our hearts by the Holy Spirit, whom he has given us.*
> Romans 5:1-5 (NIV)

According to Paul, when we approach suffering with faith we shall have peace with God and a close relationship with Jesus Christ. The blessings of grace seldom are received by those who live a life of charm, wealth, and comfort. The blessings of grace come to those who live in the reality of hope refined through challenge, adversity and suffering.

For suffering is not something that one should try to always avoid as a general life goal. Indeed, in living, one must accept suffering as part of growth and character development. Suffering may even lead us to find blessings and may help us to be able to bless others. The broken hearted are the ones who learn to deeply love. The contrite spirit is the one who is filled with a beautiful reverence of God and a peace that is given by the Holy Spirit. In His inaugural address/sermon Jesus began by saying: *"Blessed are the poor in spirit, for theirs is the Kingdom of God"* (Matthew 5:3 NIV). Some of those who heard Jesus upon this mountainside along the Sea of Galilee had climbed up bearing the pain of their infirmities. They were rewarded in their search for hope and healing by Jesus as they received the Word of God's grace and glory.

There are mountains of pain and suffering to overcome with cancer. Yet in the midst of all of this, the Spirit of God is ready to bless and guide us in the path of discovery and peace. God can move certain mountains, help us overcome other mountains, or give us peace to accept those immovable mountains. Sometimes we are like Moses, who did not cross the Jordan River, but accepted his limitations and retreated to the solitude of the mountain to die with peace and dignity. Moses trusted that the Lord was with him; very soon he was brought up to Heaven. We may grow in the journey and rejoice that eventually we shall behold God in all His glory in Heaven, and join the heavenly host in the City of God beyond this temporary earthly realm.

Later in his life and ministry the Apostle Paul wrote about the difference of viewpoint that believers develop as they move from a temporary mindset to an eternal mindset. The person who has come to believe in God and has received the gift of grace, truth, and the Holy Spirit through Jesus Christ has a new heart that is capable of constant spiritual renewal no matter what they suffer. Even those who have cancer and are physically "wasting away" may

119

experience hope and strength in the ministry of God's Spirit.

Therefore we do not lose heart. Though outwardly we are wasting away, yet inwardly we are being renewed day by day. For our light and momentary troubles are achieving for us an eternal glory that far outweighs them all. So we fix our eyes not on what is seen, but on what is unseen. For what is seen is temporary, but what is unseen is eternal.
II Corinthians 4:16-18 (NIV)

The very presence of Jesus Christ, and His very word of life and truth, gives us a firm promise of God's Kingdom to come and a greater glimpse of the eternal glory of God. Jesus has come to us, "Emmanuel", to bring peace and reconciliation to mankind. He came to earth, accepted the cross, and accomplished so great a salvation that it far outweighed any suffering that he needed to go through in order to fulfill God's plan. Therefore, we must look beyond the temporary confines of suffering in order to see the transcendent possibilities of God's Spirit at work. Suffering is therefore not necessarily a prison, but suffering through faith may be a gateway to grace and truth. In fighting cancer we must not be fixated on the cancer, but upon the One who can help us and guide us through the battle. We must trust in what is beyond the treatments and beyond our physical pain and suffering. There is another side to it all that will bring us hope, healing, and wholeness.

Paul goes on to speak about the physical bodies that we are given on this earth and the hope that we have of something greater that God is preparing.

Now we know that if the earthly tent we live in is destroyed, we have a building from God, an eternal house in heaven, not built by human hands. Meanwhile we groan, longing to be clothed with our heavenly dwelling, because when we are clothed, we will not be found naked. For while we are in this tent, we groan and are burdened, because we do not wish to

*be unclothed but to be clothed with our heavenly dwelling, so
that what is mortal may be swallowed up by life. Now it is
God who has made us for this very purpose and has given us
the Spirit as a deposit, guaranteeing what is to come.* II
Corinthians 5:1-5 (NIV)

Paul was a tentmaker, so for him it was natural to think
about our human bodies as being like tents. Tents are
temporary dwelling places; they are portable and yet
subject to wear and tear. Tents are flexible and when
anchored can endure great winds and extremes of
temperature. Yet tents have their limits, and will not
always protect you from the elements. Tents require care
and maintenance, patching and cleaning. A tent may last
for quite some years, but eventually there are things that get
into the fabric that can cause it to break down, such as mold
or mildew. So too our bodies are wonderful dwelling
places that God has created for our souls and for
community with others. Still, the present bodies we have
will go through wear and tear, and over time can develop
cancer. These bodies will eventually be destroyed, but
before they break down and we perish, our bodies will
cause us to groan and long for something better. Our
mortality can not be disguised, we are naked and vulnerable
coming into this life and this nakedness is also true as we
end our physical existence.

God has a purpose for us, and a design that involves
redemption into a resurrection body reserved for all who
long to be clothed with the heavenly dwelling/body in Jesus
Christ the risen Lord. When we die our bodies will return
to the earth, but our souls shall not be swallowed into an
abyss of nothingness. We must all appear before the Lord
our God, who is creator and redeemer. For those who have
received the deposit of God's Spirit through faith, they are
welcomed into the way that leads to life eternal. For those
who have rejected the gift of God's grace which leads to
new life in the Spirit, there is judgment that leads to

separation and punishment for sins. Those who do not allow the Savior to purge their sins through the "cleansing treatment" of the cross shall spiritually die at the "second" death (Revelation 20:11-15). For those who do trust Jesus Christ with their soul, who do lay claim to the power of the cross, Christ will radiate the very love and righteousness of God within their hearts to bring healing and new life. There is a golden thread of divine grace that connects us to God in the movement of faith that leads us to believe and trust in Jesus Christ. This golden thread of grace can lead us through darkness, suffering, and death. Connected and bound eternally by love's strong cord we are led into God's eternal Kingdom. The resurrection body to come is immortal and glorious, like that to which God gave our Savior and Lord Jesus Christ. For now we may live as citizens of that eternal Kingdom, learning the lessons of self-control as we journey in this life by faith, trust, and obedience.

One more thought on self-control and limitations I want to address, with a mix of seriousness and humor, is the issue of contact avoidance and hand sanitizing for cancer patients and their caregivers. Now, it is a big deal for people to understand that when the doctor says "You have cancer", he/she usually makes it clear that "you are not to be in direct contact with the general public, you can not go to visit anyone in the hospital or nursing home, you are to avoid going into schools or churches, and you should avoid any contact with those who are sick." Besides wondering what kind of a life you are supposed to lead, one learns to develop a strategy to deal with the fact that some contact will take place. Still you wonder, "How can I know if someone is sick? Where have they been? Will they be honest enough, or sensitive enough, not to approach me?" I found that the first thing people want to do when they hear you have cancer is hug you and make contact to support you. It is only natural, and they can't be blamed for their desire to show care. My strategy at first was to wear a mask and gloves as often as needed. I soon adapted by using hand sanitizer everywhere I went. Door knobs became spheres that harbored a world of germs. Phones became receptacles of disease and death. "The phone call is for you." "Oh Thanks a million!" When waiting in the doctor's office I refrained from picking up magazines, registration form ink pens, and from pushing elevator buttons with my finger. I developed great elbow control. Yes, I must confess, I had become a "germ-a-phobic", "paranoidal", freak. Though I hoped to exert control over what ever micro organisms I was exposed to, it became all too clear that I felt threatened by these unseen forces. In looking back it is clear that God protected me. Of course I was fighting more than the enemy of micro organisms. There was a much greater work of protection from my Lord and Savior. I have come to appreciate the unseen work of God's special agents, the angels, who though mostly unseen, act as shielding servants all about us. While my exercise of protection and self control was important, I grew to trust that ultimately God was in control, God protects us, and that includes cancer or microbes.

Through battling cancer I had learned to trust in God, make adjustments, and understand my limitations. I learned to live with an acceptance of my mortality and use this experience to deepen my faith. Furthermore, I grew to appreciate the immortality of my soul in light of God's mercy, His plan for my salvation and eternity. Through all this I came to see that suffering and pain have a purpose. In Christ I live, love, hope, and venture forward. My prayer is that if you are battling cancer, or helping someone else who is, that you will find the peace, presence and power of God in the midst of your limitations and illness. The living God of the universe calls us to discover His abundant grace, truth, and love in the midst of fighting cancer, or any other type of illness or disease. In truth, all of us have sinned and fallen short of the glory of God. This "spiritual" cancer must be recognized, repented of, and cleansed through divine forgiveness. There is one Lord and Savior that God has given for our redemption, Jesus the Christ, the Son of the living God. He is bright and glorious. I have seen the Glory of the One and only, my Lord and Savior. I am forever changed because of that cleansing encounter and experience of healing. When He placed His hands upon my shoulder and head, the energy that went through my body was awesome and powerful, healing and comforting. I was filled with His presence of perfect peace in that moment, and even now I am continually humbled as the Prince of Peace is still working through my life, transforming me from day to day.

What future can we look forward to? Will there come a time when there will be no more cancer? Will death itself be destroyed? The Apostle Paul expressed such hope as he wrote to people who were confused and concerned regarding the assurance of the resurrection and of eternal life:

> *For while we are in this tent, we groan and are burdened, because we do not wish to be unclothed but to be clothed with our heavenly dwelling, so that what is mortal may be swallowed up by life. Now it is God who has made us for this very purpose and has given us the Spirit as a deposit, guaranteeing what is to come.*
>
> 2 Corinthians 5:4-5 (NIV)

There are some who say that the hope of heaven is a fabricated idea. They can only believe what they see, looking only to the temporary elements and missing the spiritual, missing the very eternal presence of God that undergirds everything. To those who doubt I ask, what if the Apostle Paul was right? What if billions of believers in history have been right? And what if Jesus was speaking the truth by saying *"I am the way, the truth, and the life"*? (John 14:6) If the Gospel of God's revelation and gift of grace in Jesus Christ is true, then we must believe that cancer (something that is mortal) shall be "*swallowed up by life*". God chooses to clothe our dying nakedness with the spiritual garment of salvation. New life with God is possible right now by faith. Eventually God shall clothe the redeemed with a new resurrected body in heaven. Our souls shall abide in the place of heavenly dwelling that is prepared for all who believe.

Time could never allow for a satisfactory elaboration on the extent of God's Kingdom. Suffice it to say that the extent of God's Kingdom is not restricted to time or space, yet the working of God's Kingdom is also existent within this life's time and space according to the will of God. The Kingdom of God is therefore both here on earth and somewhere else in a heavenly realm, outside of us and yet by faith and grace the Kingdom of God is born within us. Jesus preached the Gospel of hope and life as He said: *"The time has come," he said. "The kingdom of God is near. Repent and believe the good news!"* (Mark 1:15 NIV)

Jesus also answered the question of where the Kingdom of God is by saying: *"The Kingdom of God is within you"* (Luke 17:20-21 NIV). There is great hope for people when it comes to experiencing God's transforming grace and love, this is true both in this life and in the life to come. The grand vision of faith that Jesus expressed in the Lord's Prayer is that God's Kingdom shall come "*on earth as it is in heaven*" (Matthew 6:10). My prayer is that God's peace and strength will help you in your particular struggle or battle with cancer. I also believe that Soul Fruit is born in adversity, and this fruit will extend into the eternal life God prepares for believers.

16. Conclusion: Significant Insights.

Expressions of love and support for those who are battling cancer are precious and long remembered. With this in mind I contacted friends and members of our church when it looked as though Thom would be able to come home for the first time after he had finished 9 weeks of intervention and treatment at the hospital. They made plans to be at our home when Thom was scheduled to arrive. People made a sign that was plastered to the side of our house and they tied orange balloons to the lamp post. Marilyn and I had painted and redecorated Thom's room in bright orange and green (his two favorite colors at that time). You could say we did a makeover of his room. In addition, we also had the whole house vent system professionally cleaned in order to make our home environmentally healthy. All systems were go. People were going to be there as we pulled in by car so as to cheer and applaud his return home. I cried with bittersweet joy as I thought of the support and love Thom would experience in coming home.

Everyone was ready, yet the chemotherapy proved to be too difficult to handle. While the doctors had given us an estimated time, now the doctors told us that he had to stay longer. So I had to call all the excited and prepared friends, and they returned home and waited for another day. It was disappointing, but a reminder of how unpredictable a fight with cancer can be.

Eventually, a few days later, Thom was able to come home. Thankfully, a few of the people who had waited before did show up to cheer his arrival. Still, it was not quite the moment we had thought it would be. Thom was still tired after the hour ride home and he was more subdued as a result. Those who came were a faithful few whose faces and voices were still much appreciated. Every gesture of love was important in the ongoing battle with cancer. It occurred to me then that, while the fight was on, it helped to look forward to that bright day in Heaven when we shall receive the applause of a great cloud of witnesses upon our homecoming. But until then, we need those faithful few who will line our pathway to cheer us on, who will understand that a battle with cancer is a marathon and so they will go with us through the various stages and times of disappointment, faith, fear, triumph, frustration, and victory. I don't think that it is possible to predict everything that a person will go through with cancer, but it is possible to believe in the ultimate result of God's grace, truth, and love. We are to pass on the torch of faith that gives hope, and so encourage one another on through life's adversity and trials. Love can triumph over anything, even cancer. God's steadfast love endures forever and ever. Some day those who venture to believe in God shall receive the applause of heaven, and shall hear the voice and see the face of the one who bore their sorrows and sins, and rose again in brilliant glory. People of faith shall see the face of Jesus, our redeemer King, whose grace carries us through cancer and suffering, and whose grace makes us acceptable, clean, and new before our creator God, the Heavenly Father.

In the life we are given, and that includes even the unusual blessing of cancer, we are to be more than conquerors through Him (Christ) who loved us. We are being prepared for an eternal Kingdom that has no end, complete with a body that shall be incorruptible, (that is, cancer free and without pain). While in this life we may indeed be signs and symbols of God's grace and truth, even with the corruptible and temporal bodies we are given. Through our faith and courage, and the values of believing and obeying God, we may represent the very Kingdom of God that is at work in us. In fact, this very presence of God's Kingdom within us is even working through us in the days we are given here on earth.

If it were not for the odd and unwelcome blessing of cancer, I may not have had the humbling and healing honor to behold my Savior Jesus face to face in this life. Now I look forward to behold His face and glory again in Heaven, and/or some day on earth. Furthermore, if it were not for the challenge of helping our son battle cancer, I may not have gained this deepened reliance of praying to God and believing in His divine intervention. If it were not for being with my grandfather, brother, and father in the last days of battling cancer, I would not have developed the same appreciation for how fragile and precious life is. Having cancer personally has taught me that this world is beautiful, yet delicate. Humility before God is born out of fragility. Being with others who are going through cancer has taught me compassion and empathy. I can see so much in every person, every moment, every gift, every struggle, every desire; and I am learning to more deeply trust and obey God so as to seek His grace and glory above my own limitations.

I truly have experienced how directly God is involved in our daily concerns, big and small. There is not one aspect of our existence that escapes His awareness. The details of fighting cancer are all within His Sovereign care and control. I cannot fully comprehend the infinite and encompassing knowledge of God, but I will always appreciate His complete personal presence and peace. The blessing of cancer has taught me to grow "Soul Fruit" as I have relied upon God even more. For this I am eternally grateful.

Will my cancer return some day? If it does will that mean that some people will no longer believe in my experience of healing? Why is healing always limited to a complete cure? Is there not a process and journey where suffering and healing coexist in a way that moves us toward God? What will I go through with treatment if my Non-Hodgkin's Lymphoma comes back? How would it differ? These questions have been part of my journey, as well as many questions related to the welfare of my wife and family, and the people in the communities and churches I am blessed to serve.

Recently I returned to Dr. Danish for a 6 month follow up visit. He indicated that my IGM level (a specific protein that is produced when my cancer is active) was elevated. "I want you to have a CT-Scan as soon as possible so we may determine if your cancer is growing." He continued to explain that the type of cancer I have had will continue to be treatable to some extent over time, but not one that will be cured. Marilyn and I realized then that while we had been given a six year reprieve from my cancer, now we probably would resume the battle. I was honestly disappointed at first, but then took heart that God would continue to bless and guide us into the future. Nonetheless, no one wants to hear that their cancer has probably returned. The prospect of going through chemotherapy again is not easy to accept, however, one does have a better understanding of what the battle will be like and how to deal with it.

Ten days after I had the CT-Scan of my abdomen, the results were good. There was no evidence of the cancer being on the move again. Praise God! When we saw Dr. Danish he said: "You're alright. We'll check again through blood tests in three months and do a CT-Scan in a year. Take care!" Once again, I rejoiced in the grace of God. My family and our church family were thankful and relieved. The peace of Christ restored my sense of purpose in living longer so as to serve and care for others. My hope and prayer is to be able to speak to people about cancer, and I pray this book will be shared with many. This was realized at first recently, following my good news, as I spoke to the Rotary club I belong to about supporting those who are gong through cancer. I was humbled by their support and applause. My prayer is that God can use me as long as I have breath and strength.

While I am challenged with the realization that I will live with cancer for the rest of my days, and at times I will likely face my adversary again. I choose to see this not as a curse, but instead I choose to see this as a blessing. The blessing is that I will be kept mindful of how precious life is, and of how reliant I am upon my Creator/Redeemer. After all, healing is temporary, compared with the final hope I have in the resurrection and eternal life given through my Lord and Savior Jesus Christ.

When it comes to reliance, I have come to a realization of how critical it is to live at a healthier pace, one in which we respect our boundaries and live within our physical limitations. God speaks to us through His Holy Spirit when it involves counsel and guidance in the decisions we make and life we lead. Many times when we push ourselves too hard, or delay or deny medical help, it is because we are being disobedient to the leading of God's Holy Spirit and His word of counsel. God speaks constantly and consistently to our hearts and minds related to His concern for us; and if we are listening we will hear and respond to His voice.

Along with this, God works and speaks through those to whom He has given understanding and knowledge, and it is always wise to heed the advice of those whom God has equipped through medical training and wisdom. This does not deny the supernatural intervention of God for healing; it affirms that God is involved in all true knowledge and in every matter. We can learn a great deal from cases where a cure is not found or healing involves something different than the physical extension of our lives. The pace of someone who sees life anew, and gains an awareness of their mortality, can even provide a perspective that is both realistic and liberating. For many cancer survivors and supporters, they are highly aware that each day is a gift, and each moment is to be cherished. The priorities of life are adjusted when we face our mortality. In this temporal life we are given the opportunity to live fruitfully as citizens of God's Kingdom. We all must carefully weigh over the significance of our decisions and actions. Is it our desire is to make it all count, to become a blessing to others? My personal desire and prayer is to be faithful to share my story of God's healing love, be truthful to my limits, sensitive to God's leading, and available to what God is teaching me in this journey with cancer.

To the point, cancer challenges our assumptions of hope, and calls forth our resources of faith. God calls us to discover His presence in the various challenges that we will encounter with the wondrous, yet fragile, life we are given. If we place our ultimate hope in that which will pass away, even our very bodies, then we have misplaced our hope toward that which is temporal. If cancer can make our mortality and corruptibility quite clear, then it is a servant to teach us to place our ultimate hope in God. Our hope is not only in the eternal life to come, but in the blessings that are found in every aspect of the journey of life where God is present and powerful. For me, I have experienced the blessings of how God has revealed His power and grace while I have dealt with the effects of this disease. I have grown closer to God while in this journey with cancer. I take heart that I am not alone as I embrace the words of my Savior who said: "*I am with you always, even to the end of the age.*"

Will my life be shortened by cancer? Probably it will be. Has my life been blessed by a realization that there is nothing that can separate me from the love of God? Yes. Cancer is there to remind me that I can not boast in my own strength or resources. For God is the solid rock, my Creator and Redeemer, and my journey will not end with cancer. Life will continue for eternity with salvation and hope, light and love. I trust my Lord Jesus who shall lead me to heaven's home. My soul shall receive a new resurrection body that neither cancer nor sin can spoil. The fruit of my soul shall give glory to God from whom all blessings abound.

The Journey is Blessed

The journey is blessed
When from the ground of our adversity
Blossoms come forth within our souls

Bearing tried fruit that has seen pain
Withstood suffering
What taste is pure joy
The fragrance of which is priceless peace

The fruit of God's grace is pleasing and right
Come and be blessed
In the garden of God's love and delight

Scott T. Arnold
2009

The Arnold family, Fall 2008

Thom and "Rita"

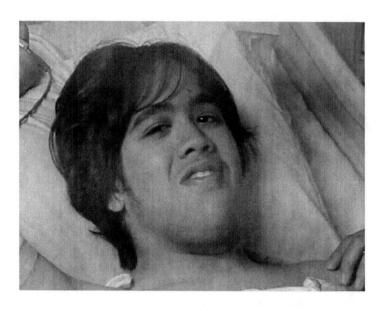

Thom in the hospital before chemotherapy.

Thom in the midst of chemotherapy.